MINISTRY OF DEFENCE

Recruitment and Retention in the Armed Forces: Detailed Survey Results and Case Studies

This volume is published alongside a first volume comprising
the Comptroller and Auditor General's report
Ministry of Defence: Recruitment and Retention in the Armed Forces,
HC 1633-I Session 2005-06

LONDON: The Stationery Off¹
£13.50

Ordered by the
House of Commons
to be printed on 31 October 2006

REPORT BY THE COMPTROLLER AND AUDITOR GENERAL | HC 1633-II Session 2005-2006 | 3 November 2006

This report has been prepared under Section 6 of the National Audit Act 1983 for presentation to the House of Commons in accordance with Section 9 of the Act.

John Bourn
Comptroller and Auditor General
National Audit Office

31 October 2006

The National Audit Office study team consisted of:

Steve Merrifield, Albert Hong, Bill New, Kirsten Payne, Alison Smith, Katherine Stone and Brigadier (Retired) John Baker MBE, under the direction of Mark Andrews

This report can be found on the National Audit Office web site at www.nao.org.uk

For further information about the National Audit Office please contact:

National Audit Office
Press Office
157-197 Buckingham Palace Road
Victoria
London
SW1W 9SP

Tel: 020 7798 7400

Email: enquiries@nao.gsi.gov.uk

CONTENTS

INTRODUCTION

1   This Volume (Volume 2) of the Report is in two parts. The first part contains detailed results from the National Audit Office survey of current and former personnel in a selection of pinch point trades.

2   The second part contains case studies examining 11 pinch point trades in detail. These are:

■   Royal Navy: Nuclear Watchkeepers (Marine Engineering Artificer MEA(SM)).

■   Royal Navy: Warfare Branch (General Service) Leading Hands.

■   Royal Navy: Royal Marines Other Ranks (General Duties).

■   Army: Recovery Mechanic (Royal Electrical and Mechanical Engineers).

■   Army: Ammunition Technician (Royal Logistic Corps).

■   Army: Information Systems Engineer (Royal Signals).

■   Army: Explosive Ordnance Disposal (Royal Engineers).

■   Royal Air Force: Weapons System Operator (Linguist).

■   Royal Air Force: General Technician Electrical.

■   Tri-Service: General Practitioners.

■   Tri-Service: Accident and Emergency and Intensive Therapy Unit Nurses.

3   Each of the case studies examines the reasons why the trade has become an operational pinch point, the current manning situation, the impact of increased operational commitments on personnel in the trade, the initiatives the Department has in place to improve manning and to relieve pressures on personnel, and when the Department believes the trade will no longer be considered an operational pinch point.

DETAILED SURVEY RESULTS

1   This Appendix sets out the key findings from our survey of former and serving personnel from a selection of pinch point trades. The total of the replies received for sub-groups is less than the total of the replies from all

respondents, as some respondents did not state which sub-group they belonged to. Percentages may not add up to 100 per cent due to rounding and a small number who did not give an answer.

	Royal Navy	Royal Marines	Army	Royal Air Force	All
Current Personnel					
Total replies received	1,164	217	1,414	1,785	4,695
Rank					
Officer[1]	0%	0%	0%	30%	12%
Non-Commissioned Officer/Warrant Officer/ Senior Rate	65%	54%	76%	40%	58%
Other Rank/Junior Rate	35%	45%	23%	29%	30%
Length of Service					
Less than 1 year	0%	2%	0%	1%	0%
1 – 2 years	0%	6%	3%	4%	3%
2 – 5 years	5%	17%	12%	15%	12%
5 – 10 years	18%	20%	25%	19%	20%
10 – 15 years	15%	14%	21%	12%	15%
15 – 20 years	31%	22%	29%	26%	28%
20 years +	31%	19%	10%	24%	21%

	Royal Navy	Royal Marines	Army	Royal Air Force	All
Current Personnel *continued*					
Current engagement ends					
Within the next 6 months	3%	3%	4%	3%	3%
6 months – 1 year	5%	6%	7%	4%	5%
1 – 2 years	8%	6%	10%	8%	9%
2 – 5 years	21%	25%	22%	30%	25%
5 – 10 years	34%	20%	21%	35%	29%
10 – 15 years	21%	15%	19%	14%	18%
15 – 20 years	6%	18%	11%	3%	7%
20 years+	1%	6%	4%	2%	3%
Gender					
Male	96%	97%	88%	92%	92%
Female	4%	2%	12%	8%	8%
Age					
Under 20	0%	3%	1%	1%	1%
20 – 24	5%	20%	13%	13%	11%
25 – 29	15%	18%	21%	16%	17%
30 – 34	26%	19%	29%	18%	23%
35 – 39	31%	24%	28%	26%	28%
40+	23%	16%	8%	26%	19%
Marital Status					
Single	10%	17%	16%	16%	15%
In a relationship (not living together)	7%	13%	12%	10%	10%
Married/Living with a partner	75%	62%	64%	68%	68%
Separated/Divorced	7%	7%	7%	5%	6%
Widowed	0%	1%	0%	0%	0%
Children					
Yes	62%	49%	49%	52%	54%
No	37%	51%	50%	47%	46%
Former Personnel					
Total replies received	227	193	162	177	761
Rank on leaving the Services					
Officer[1]	0%	0%	0%	27%	6%
Non-Commissioned Officer/Warrant Officer/Senior Rate	61%	37%	79%	43%	55%
Other Rank/Junior Rate	38%	61%	21%	27%	38%

	Royal Navy	Royal Marines	Army	Royal Air Force	All
Former Personnel *continued*					
Length of time since leaving					
Less than 1 year	32%	26%	43%	40%	34%
1 – 2 years	48%	53%	43%	41%	47%
More than 2 years	20%	21%	15%	19%	19%
Length of time spent in the Services					
1 – 2 years	0%	1%	1%	1%	1%
2 – 5 years	4%	27%	8%	12%	12%
5 – 10 years	25%	32%	28%	12%	25%
10 – 15 years	11%	6%	9%	10%	9%
15 – 20 years	1%	2%	5%	12%	5%
20 years +	58%	32%	49%	52%	48%
Method of leaving the Services					
Applying for voluntary outflow	51%	57%	32%	46%	47%
At end of engagement	38%	31%	52%	38%	39%
Not asked to re-engage	2%	0%	1%	5%	2%
Voluntary redundancy	4%	5%	1%	1%	3%
Compulsory redundancy	0%	0%	1%	1%	0%
Other	5%	7%	12%	8%	8%
Gender					
Male	98%	99%	93%	90%	96%
Female	2%	0%	7%	10%	4%
Age					
20 – 24	3%	20%	6%	7%	9%
25 – 29	18%	33%	20%	14%	21%
30 – 34	17%	12%	15%	10%	14%
35 – 39	4%	3%	7%	12%	6%
40+	59%	31%	51%	57%	50%
Marital Status					
Single	8%	16%	10%	12%	12%
In a relationship (not living together)	6%	7%	6%	4%	6%
Married/Living with a partner	79%	73%	77%	78%	77%
Separated/Divorced	6%	4%	8%	6%	6%
Widowed	0%	0%	0%	0%	1%
Children					
Yes	59%	41%	51%	61%	53%
No	41%	59%	49%	39%	47%

Expectations and Experiences of a Service career

	Royal Navy	Royal Marines	Army	Royal Air Force	All	Former personnel
Reasons for joining						
Total replies received	1,164	217	1,414	1,785	4,695	761
Percentage rating factors as 'very important' or 'important' in their decision to join the Services						
Interesting work	91%	93%	95%	94%	94%	92%
Opportunities to travel	86%	91%	86%	85%	86%	90%
Challenging work	80%	91%	87%	87%	85%	84%
Job Security	87%	78%	82%	85%	84%	79%
Excitement	81%	93%	86%	84%	84%	84%
Variety of work	77%	84%	83%	85%	82%	83%
Sport/active lifestyle	72%	91%	82%	80%	79%	80%
Opportunity to do something worthwhile	72%	80%	78%	83%	78%	78%
Opportunities to gain qualifications and trade specific skills	76%	63%	81%	73%	76%	69%
Pension	82%	67%	73%	76%	76%	67%
Pay and allowances	79%	62%	75%	75%	75%	67%
Promotion Opportunities	79%	62%	72%	73%	74%	68%
Comradeship	63%	80%	71%	75%	71%	76%
Opportunity to go on operations	47%	85%	60%	57%	56%	59%
Family tradition	22%	22%	23%	23%	23%	20%
Overall experience						
View on Service career (to date for current personnel)						
Significantly better than expected	6%	7%	6%	6%	6%	15%
Better than expected	26%	30%	31%	31%	30%	32%
As I expected it to be	38%	38%	35%	36%	36%	33%
Worse than expected	26%	19%	23%	23%	23%	16%
Significantly worse than expected	4%	5%	4%	4%	4%	3%

NOTE
1 All but one of the trades we surveyed were Other Ranks trades.

2   Main satisfaction factors shows the top 12 factors where more than 50 per cent of current and more than 64 per cent of former personnel said they were 'satisfied' or 'very satisfied'.

3   Main dissatisfaction factors shows the top 12 factors where more than 30 per cent of current personnel or more than 32 per cent of former personnel said they were 'dissatisfied' or 'very dissatisfied'.

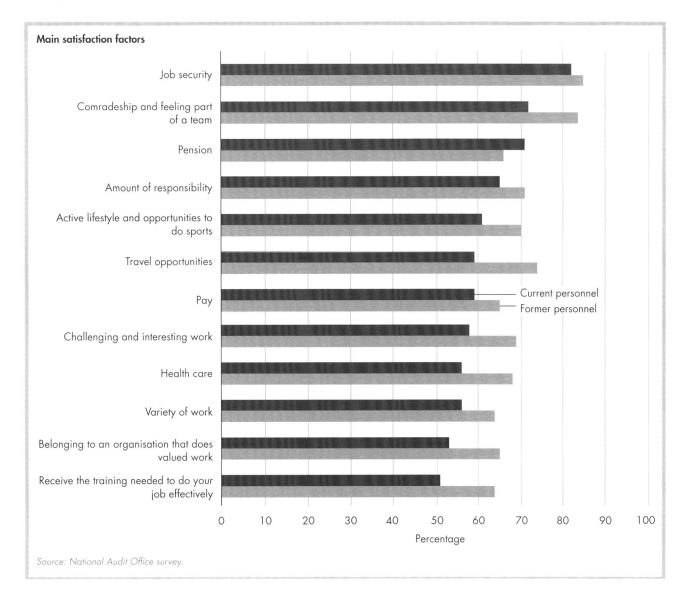

Main satisfaction factors

Source: National Audit Office survey.

Main dissatisfaction factors

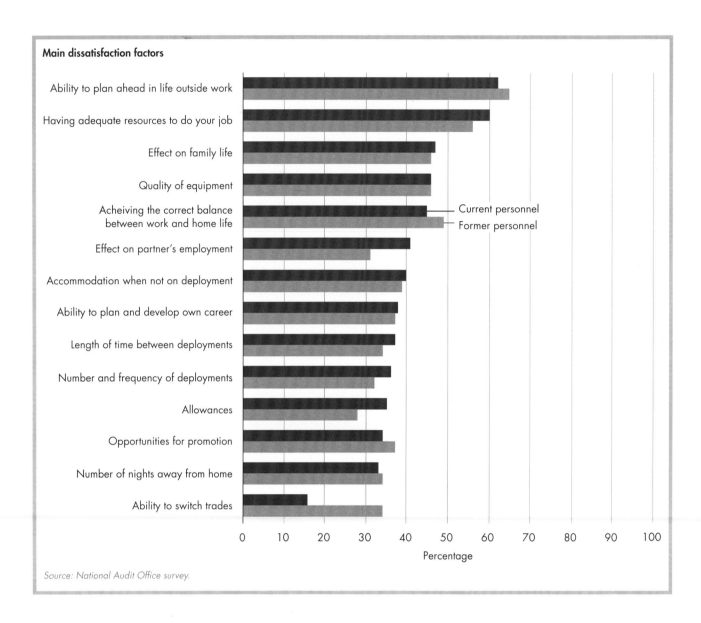

Source: National Audit Office survey.

Career intentions – current personnel

	Royal Navy	Royal Marines	Army	Royal Air Force	All
Total replies received	1,164	217	1,414	1,785	4,695
Current intentions towards length of Service career					
Intend to serve full Service career	45%	45%	57%	31%	43%
Intend to re-engage but not yet decided on full Service career	4%	5%	3%	8%	6%
Intend to serve until the end of current engagement	17%	10%	6%	28%	17%
Given notice to leave at end of current engagement	2%	2%	2%	2%	2%
Intend to leave when another job becomes available	5%	4%	3%	3%	4%
Intend to leave before end of current engagement	8%	10%	6%	7%	7%
Given notice to leave before end of current engagement	4%	3%	4%	4%	4%
Undecided	15%	20%	17%	16%	16%
Percentage looking for jobs outside the Services					
Not interested in looking for another job	21%	26%	22%	26%	24%
Not actively looking, but might be interested if the right job came along	29%	33%	26%	26%	27%
Occasionally look at job adverts but have not acted on any	26%	20%	26%	29%	27%
Have sent for information about jobs	16%	13%	16%	11%	14%
Actively applying for jobs outside the Services	7%	7%	9%	8%	8%
Don't know/not stated	1%	0%	1%	1%	1%

Reasons for leaving *(continued)*

	Royal Navy	Royal Marines	Army	Royal Air Force	All	Former personnel
Quality of welfare support for families	23%	25%	31%	30%	28%	18%
Workload when not on operational deployments too heavy	34%	20%	25%	27%	28%	17%
Unable to gain experience in field of choice	19%	20%	36%	27%	27%	16%
Quality of operational welfare support	26%	28%	28%	25%	27%	16%
Not enough responsibility	16%	20%	32%	27%	25%	16%
Quality of accommodation on operational deployment	30%	23%	19%	23%	24%	16%
Workload on operational deployments too heavy	30%	13%	19%	20%	22%	14%
Dissatisfaction with pension	30%	20%	12%	18%	20%	7%
Workload when not on operational deployment too light	4%	8%	19%	12%	12%	6%
Inability to change trade	13%	35%	13%	9%	13%	12%
Inability to transfer to another Service	11%	23%	12%	6%	10%	7%
Not deployed often enough	4%	28%	11%	9%	9%	9%
Too much responsibility	9%	0%	7%	8%	7%	4%
Workload on operational deployments too light	6%	8%	5%	4%	5%	4%
Too much time at home when not on deployments	5%	0%	3%	3%	4%	2%
Operational deployments are too short	2%	5%	3%	2%	2%	2%

	Likely to reconsider	Neither likely nor unlikely	Unlikely to reconsider	Don't know
Current personnel intending to leave (791 responses)				
Likelihood of factors to persuade to stay				
Better ability to plan life/career	63%	16%	10%	11%
Financial incentives	61%	15%	13%	11%
Offered a posting of my choice	52%	22%	15%	11%
More time at home between deployments	44%	29%	15%	12%
Promotion opportunities	43%	27%	19%	12%
Shorter periods of separation	42%	30%	16%	12%
Fewer periods of separation	40%	31%	17%	12%
Improved equipment/technology	39%	31%	18%	12%
Improvements in welfare	31%	36%	20%	12%
Further career training	30%	38%	19%	12%
Improved support for families	27%	39%	22%	12%
Opportunity to transfer trade groups	10%	40%	37%	13%
Opportunity to transfer to another Service	10%	38%	39%	13%
Nothing would persuade me to stay	13%			

Retention Incentives

	Royal Navy	Royal Marines	Army	Royal Air Force	All
Total replies received	1,164	217	1,414	1,785	4,695
Percentage offered financial incentives					
Yes	24%	14%	25%	13%	20%
No	74%	81%	74%	85%	79%
Don't know	2%	4%	3%	1%	2%

	All
Total offered Financial Incentives	917
Influence on decision to stay	
Persuaded me to stay	11%
Had some influence but was not the deciding factor	27%
No impact, as I would have stayed anyway	53%
No impact, as I am still planning to leave	3%
Don't know	6%

	4,695
Current Personnel	4,695
Other incentives offered to persuade to stay in the Services	Offered
Promotion opportunities	12%
Posting of their choice	8%
Further career training	6%
Opportunity to transfer trade groups	4%
Better ability to plan life/career	3%
Opportunity to transfer to another Service	1%
Shorter periods of separation	1%
Fewer periods of separation	1%
More time at home when not on deployments	1%
Other	1%
None of the above	61%
Don't know	15%

Retention Incentives *(continued)*

	Royal Navy	Royal Marines	Army	Royal Air Force	All
Former Personnel					
Total who took the decision to leave voluntarily	210 (93%)	179 (93%)	138 (85%)	152 (86%)	681 (89%)
Efforts made by the Services to persuade personnel to stay					
Yes, great efforts were made	9%	18%	14%	6%	11%
Yes, some effort was made	46%	47%	24%	24%	37%
No, no effort was made	30%	21%	26%	48%	31%
Not stated	15%	14%	36%	22%	21%
Opportunities and incentives offered					
Promotion	14%	37%	20%	8%	20%
Posting of choice	4%	11%	10%	7%	8%
Further career training	6%	11%	10%	7%	8%
Financial incentives	10%	5%	2%	3%	5%
Better ability to plan life/career	6%	3%	2%	5%	4%
Opportunity to transfer trade groups	3%	5%	1%	1%	3%
Shorter periods of separation	3%	0%	1%	2%	2%
Fewer periods of separation	2%	1%	2%	4%	2%
More time at home between deployments	4%	1%	1%	3%	2%
Opportunity to transfer to another Service	1%	2%	1%	0%	1%
Improved equipment/technology	0%	0%	0%	1%	0%
Other	10%	6%	7%	7%	8%

Retention Incentives *(continued)*

	Likely to reconsider	Neither likely nor unlikely	Unlikely to reconsider	Not stated
Those who took the decision to leave voluntarily (681 responses)				
Likelihood of factors to have encouraged respondents to stay				
Better ability to plan life/career	55%	15%	7%	23%
Financial incentives	46%	17%	14%	23%
Offered a posting of my choice	42%	23%	11%	24%
More time at home between deployments	41%	24%	12%	23%
Promotion opportunities	36%	28%	13%	23%
Shorter periods of separation	36%	25%	15%	23%
Fewer periods of separation	34%	27%	15%	24%
Improved equipment/technology	33%	27%	16%	23%
Further career training	27%	35%	15%	24%
Improvements in welfare	23%	33%	20%	24%
Improved support for families	21%	34%	21%	24%
Opportunity to transfer trade groups	11%	35%	30%	24%
Opportunity to transfer to another Service	7%	32%	36%	25%
Nothing would have persuaded me to stay	11%			

Operational Deployments

	Royal Navy	Royal Marines	Army	Royal Air Force	All	Former personnel
Total replies received	1,164	217	1,414	1,785	4,695	761
Operational deployments during Service career						
0	2%	15%	7%	11%	8%	3%
1 – 2	5%	15%	24%	20%	17%	16%
3 – 5	16%	27%	36%	34%	30%	31%
6 – 10	29%	22%	27%	27%	27%	24%
11 – 15	18%	10%	5%	5%	8%	8%
16 – 20	13%	2%	1%	1%	4%	6%
20+	16%	5%	1%	1%	5%	10%
Don't know/not stated	1%	2%	0%	0%	1%	1%
Total deployed	1,124 (97%)	177 (82%)	1,309 (93%)	1,579 (88%)	4,296 (92%)	727 (96%)
Approximate length of time on operational deployments during Service career						
0 – 6 months	3%	6%	8%	9%	7%	7%
7 – 12 months	6%	15%	14%	18%	13%	13%
1 – 2 years	16%	36%	30%	41%	31%	24%
3 – 5 years	34%	28%	35%	28%	32%	27%
5 years +	40%	14%	12%	3%	16%	26%
Time between deployments						
Too long	6%	12%	10%	5%	7%	8%
About right	52%	60%	51%	48%	51%	59%
Too short	40%	23%	37%	46%	40%	29%
Don't know	2%	5%	2%	1%	2%	4%
Views on pressure on time when on deployments during the last few years						
More pressure	81%	63%	71%	73%	74%	57%
No change	17%	33%	25%	25%	23%	38%
Less pressure	1%	2%	2%	2%	2%	2%
Don't know	1%	3%	2%	1%	1%	3%

Operational Deployments *(continued)*

Extent to which number/frequency of deployments a factor in any decision to leave the Services

Career Intentions	Serve full career/re-engage	Serve until/given notice to leave at end of current engagement	Leave before end of current engagement /when another job available/given notice to leave early	Former personnel
Number of personnel	2,148	837	622	727
No impact	21%	16%	19%	49%
Some impact, but not the key factor	42%	39%	39%	27%
Big impact, too many operational deployments	34%	42%	39%	19%
Big impact, too few operational deployments	2%	2%	3%	3%
Not stated	1%	1%	1%	2%

Extent to which length of deployments a factor in any decision to leave the Services

Career Intentions	Serve full career/re-engage	Serve until/given notice to leave at end of current engagement	Leave before end of current engagement /when another job available/given notice to leave early	Former personnel
Number of personnel	2,148	837	622	727
No impact	22%	20%	22%	53%
Some impact, but not the key factor	50%	49%	42%	29%
Big impact, operational deployments too long	27%	30%	33%	16%
Big impact, operational deployments too short	1%	0%	1%	0%
Not stated	1%	1%	1%	2%

Operational Deployments *(continued)*

	Royal Navy	Royal Marines	Army	Royal Air Force	All	Former personnel
Total replies received	1,164	217	1,414	1,785	4,695	761
Views on amount of time away from home when not on operational deployment						
Too little	3%	7%	4%	4%	4%	4%
About right	54%	56%	60%	69%	62%	59%
Too much	42%	33%	34%	25%	32%	34%
Don't know	1%	5%	2%	2%	2%	3%
Views on amount of pressure on time when not on deployments during the last few years						
More pressure	76%	57%	67%	71%	71%	55%
No change	20%	32%	27%	25%	25%	35%
Less pressure	3%	5%	4%	1%	3%	7%
Don't know	1%	6%	1%	2%	2%	2%

Impact of operational deployment in various theatres on intentions to stay/leave the Services (Current personnel only)

	Number deployed	More likely to stay	No impact on decision	More likely to leave
Iraq	2,671	16%	56%	27%
Falkland Islands	1,889	12%	70%	18%
Afghanistan	1,063	17%	66%	17%
Balkans	1,955	20%	71%	9%
Africa	867	22%	70%	8%
Northern Ireland	1,565	28%	65%	7%
United Nations: Other	1,022	23%	72%	6%
United Nations: Cyprus	739	32%	64%	3%

Impact of operational deployment in various theatres on decision to leave the Services (former personnel only)

	Number deployed	No impact on decision	Somewhat more likely to leave	Definitely more likely to leave
Iraq	397	71%	15%	14%
Afghanistan	162	81%	13%	6%
Falkland Islands	330	86%	10%	4%
Balkans	284	89%	6%	5%
Africa	127	90%	9%	2%
Northern Ireland	283	90%	7%	3%
United Nations: Other	145	91%	6%	3%
United Nations: Cyprus	96	96%	2%	2%

Former Personnel - Experience since leaving the Services

	Royal Navy	Royal Marines	Army	Royal Air Force	All
Total replies received	227	193	162	177	761
Current employment status					
Full time employment	82%	67%	79%	73%	75%
Part time employment	2%	4%	2%	5%	3%
Self employed	10%	21%	10%	10%	13%
Full or part time education	2%	5%	4%	1%	3%
Unemployed/not working	3%	3%	4%	9%	4%
Total employed	213	176	148	155	694
Link between current job and Service career					
Using all or most of the skills acquired in the Services	26%	16%	33%	30%	26%
Using some of the skills, but not all	42%	39%	48%	49%	44%
Not using skills acquired in Services	31%	45%	18%	21%	30%
Ease of finding employment					
Easier than expected	54%	42%	54%	54%	51%
As expected	23%	41%	24%	30%	29%
Harder than expected	22%	16%	22%	15%	19%
Method of finding employment					
Headhunted/approached by employer	10%	9%	15%	8%	11%
Through the resettlement process	6%	4%	4%	5%	5%
Through a friend or colleague	13%	22%	16%	10%	15%
Found my job myself	71%	64%	64%	75%	68%
Total replies received	227	193	162	177	761
Comparison of civilian working life to Services					
Better than Service life	61%	44%	55%	51%	53%
Different, but no better or worse	30%	39%	28%	33%	33%
Worse than Service life	7%	14%	15%	12%	12%

Former Personnel - Experience since leaving the Services *continued*

	Much better	A little better	Neither better nor worse	A little worse	Much worse	Not applicable/ not stated
Total replies received	761					
How aspects of civilian life compare to Service life						
Having enough time to spend with family	66%	13%	11%	2%	1%	6%
Length of time away from home on business	60%	13%	20%	2%	1%	4%
Number of commitments away from home	52%	15%	27%	2%	1%	4%
Working hours	40%	21%	21%	11%	3%	3%
Pay	29%	13%	20%	22%	13%	4%
Interesting work	22%	20%	37%	12%	6%	3%
Making the best use of your skills and abilities	24%	18%	38%	10%	7%	3%
Career opportunities	21%	17%	39%	12%	7%	4%
Social life	18%	17%	35%	20%	7%	4%
Receiving the training you need to do your job effectively	18%	15%	46%	11%	6%	4%
Allowances	18%	13%	32%	17%	15%	4%
Relationships with colleagues	8%	9%	58%	17%	5%	4%
Job security	6%	5%	45%	26%	14%	4%

	Royal Navy	Royal Marines	Army	Royal Air Force	All
Total replies received	227	193	162	177	761
Regrets about decision to leave					
No regrets whatsoever	46%	34%	34%	45%	40%
A few, but on balance I made the right decision	44%	48%	48%	37%	44%
Several, I'm not sure if I made the right decision	3%	11%	6%	5%	6%
Yes, I regret my decision to leave	3%	4%	6%	7%	5%
Not stated	4%	2%	7%	5%	4%
Likelihood of rejoining the Services					
Likely	7%	8%	8%	8%	8%
Unlikely	86%	80%	83%	81%	83%
Don't know/undecided	5%	10%	7%	7%	7%
Not stated	2%	2%	2%	3%	2%
Percentage approached by Services about rejoining					
Yes	9%	17%	9%	2%	9%
No	90%	83%	88%	96%	89%

CASE STUDY ONE
Royal Navy Nuclear Watchkeepers –
Marine Engineering Artificer MEA (Submariner)

1   Nuclear Watchkeepers are essential to the operation of the United Kingdom's fleet of nuclear powered submarines. They have three main roles: maintaining and operating the nuclear plant including the power and propulsion systems, watch-keeping on board the submarine on a rotation basis, and support roles ashore – for example carrying out repairs in a Fleet Maintenance Unit. There are three categories of Nuclear Watchkeeper, with different levels of qualifications and experience. The Royal Navy's pinch point trade is the more senior Category A and Category B qualified Nuclear Watchkeepers.

2   Those currently serving as Nuclear Watchkeepers joined the Royal Navy as Marine Engineering Artificers, and qualified as Nuclear Watchkeepers after a number of years:

- Four year engineering apprenticeship followed by a further period of training and experience on submarines, including training in operating nuclear plant.

- Qualify as Category C Nuclear Watchkeeper Petty Officer rank (after five to six years).

- Spend a number of years at sea as Category C before being able to qualify as Category B Watchkeepers and gain promotion to Chief Petty Officer.

- Category B Watchkeepers qualify in either the electrical or mechanical specialism, or can become dual qualified in both. They must become qualified in both to be considered for further promotion (to Category A).

- Category A Watchkeepers are Warrant Officers, the highest qualified supervisory ratings, with many years experience. Certain duties and responsibilities on submarines, such as Officer of the Watch and the highest-level maintenance can only be done by Category A Watchkeepers.

Costs of recruiting and training are not available at trade level for this specialisation.

3 The Engineering Branch within the Royal Navy is being restructured under the Navy Board Personnel Change Programme. The current Artificer and Mechanic 'streams'[1] are being replaced with a single Engineering Technician career path, and periods of training will alternate with time spent gaining experience at sea, rather than the current system whereby most training is received upfront. Marine Engineering (Submarines) will be a sub-specialism within the new Branch Structure.

Nuclear Watchkeepers manning

4 Category A and Category B Nuclear Watchkeepers are one of Royal Navy's top pinch point trades. At April 2006, there was a 29 per cent shortfall.

Why is this trade an operational pinch point?

5 Manning difficulties with the Nuclear Watchkeeper trade stem back to cutbacks in recruitment in the 1990s, as the Royal Navy reduced in size following the 'Options for Change' defence structure review in 1990. The reduced recruitment from 1992 to 1996 has created a 'black hole' in the manning profile across the Royal Navy. Redundancies were also used to cut numbers, which added to the manning shortfalls. Recruitment did not

recover completely and the Royal Navy had problems attracting sufficient people into the Submarine Service. The Royal Navy failed to meet their targets for recruits joining the trained strength in the five years leading up to 2002. Some of those who did join the Submarine Service were non-volunteers.

6 Rates of early exits also increased during this period; the shortage of manpower meant an increased burden on those who stayed in terms of more time away, increased workload, diminished shore support and disruption to their ability to plan life outside work, which in turn caused more people to apply to leave early, thus exacerbating the problems. Voluntary outflow for both Category B and Category A Nuclear Watchkeepers has fallen following the implementation of the recommendations from the 2002 Submarine Manning and Retention Review, and are currently below the Royal Navy's guidelines (**Figure 1**). However, the first people to take up the financial retention incentive introduced following this review will reach the end of their return of service period in 2007 and will therefore have their first opportunity to apply to leave early in April 2006. It is not known what impact this will have on voluntary outflow figures. Currently those who leave mainly go to civilian contractors in the Defence industry, or to jobs in nuclear decommissioning, and any decision on a resumption of the civil nuclear programme would mean increased demand for skills outside the Royal Navy.

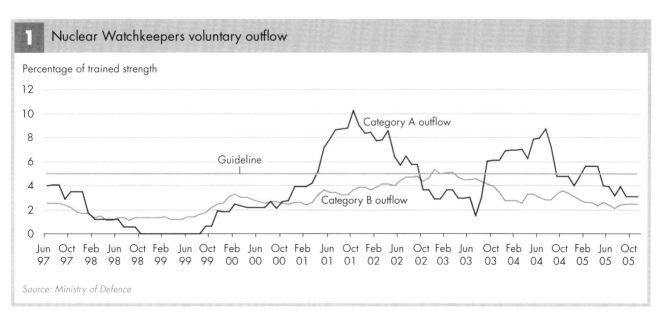

1 Nuclear Watchkeepers voluntary outflow

Source: Ministry of Defence

1 The Artificer (Technician) stream has a higher academic entry requirement, whereas those who join the Mechanic stream do not require formal qualifications (although all recruits must pass the Royal Navy's selection tests).

7   The length of time and level of experience required to become a Category B and Category A Watchkeeper means that they cannot be easily or quickly replaced. There is no shortage of Category C Watchkeepers, from which to 'grow' Category B Watchkeepers, however the smaller submarine fleet means that there are limited sea postings available for them to gain the requisite experience. This limit on progression to Category B in turn means that the pool from which to promote to Category A is reduced. In addition, some Category B Watchkeepers are reluctant to be promoted, even if they have the required dual qualifications, as they do not want the added responsibilities and workload. In 2004-05, 11 of 26 suitable candidates who were offered promotion to Warrant Officer turned this down.

Operational commitments

8   The Royal Navy is meeting all its current commitments, and harmony guidelines are not being broken. However, the manning shortages mean that some posts are "gapped", and 100 per cent manning at sea is not always being achieved. A Capability Management Team within the Naval Manning Authority is responsible for micro-managing the Nuclear Watchkeepers to ensure submarines are as fully manned as possible.

9   The impact of "gapped" posts on submarines is twofold. Firstly, those who are deployed will have an increased workload in order to cover all tasks. Some watchkeeping duties can be carried out by Mechanics in order to relieve some of the pressures on Nuclear Watchkeepers, but these personnel are not qualified to do any of the high-level maintenance. Secondly, there is a constant need to juggle deployable personnel, and in some cases to deploy them at relatively short notice, in order to fill gapped posts. This has an impact on personnel's ability to plan their lives. Nuclear Watchkeepers may be moved from submarines based alongside in port in order to fill posts at sea, which in turn leaves these roles gapped, increases workloads, and impacts negatively on work-life balance.

10   In the United Kingdom, many personnel are working long hours in order to cover all the work, and may not be able to go home every night. Problems with facilities in port, including difficulties getting stores and equipment (known as 'harbour hassle'), combined with the lack of manpower, the long hours and disruption to home life, are the biggest sources of dissatisfaction amongst Nuclear Watchkeepers.

Initiatives in place

11   The Department commissioned the Submarine Manning and Retention Review in 2002, which looked at the reasons for manning difficulties across the Submarine Service. The review recognised that pay was only part of the solution. However the critical nature of some of the shortages led to financial retention incentives being introduced for three groups, including Category B Nuclear Watchkeepers, as an urgent stop-gap measure to improve retention, whilst the real causes of discontent could be addressed.

12   The Category B Nuclear Watchkeeper financial retention incentive of £25,000 is payable to all those who gain a dual Category B qualification. It was also paid to those who already held this qualification. This was offered for a three year period from April 2003, later extended to a five year period to allow Category C Watchkeepers about to start their four to five year dual Category B training to qualify. Award of the financial retention incentive was conditional on completing a four year return of service. Eighty-nine per cent of those eligible took up the offer. Category A Watchkeepers received a 20 per cent increase in Nuclear Propulsion Pay in order to reduce the risk of divisiveness between the two populations.

13   Voluntary outflow has fallen from 4.7 per cent to around 3.2 per cent (as at April 2006) since the financial retention incentive was introduced, and the population of Category B Watchkeepers has stabilised. Although there was an initial increase in numbers attending courses to gain dual qualification, the financial retention incentive has had less success in encouraging people to move through the system to Warrant Officer and Category A Watchkeeper, for the reasons outlined earlier. Manning in both Category B and Category A is still a concern.

14   A series of non-financial initiatives were also introduced to try and address some of the underlying causes of poor retention, including work-life balance and 'harbour hassle'. These include improvements in communication and welfare, and to facilities and support provided when submarines are alongside in port. Although some progress has been made, the continuing manning shortages and resultant gapping mean that the initiatives have had limited effect so far. Our survey found that, four years on from the Submarine Manning and Retention Review, Nuclear Watchkeepers are still very unhappy with the ability to plan life, work-life balance, workload and the lack of resources to do their jobs. The replacement of Long Service at Sea Bonus with the Longer Separation Allowance is also causing resentment among Nuclear Watchkeepers who responded.

15   Currently 15 per cent of the Nuclear Watchkeeper population are ex-Regulars re-employed on Full Time Reserve Service contracts, which helps to meet some of the manning gaps, particularly in submarine decommissioning and training. Medically downgraded personnel can also be used to fill some of the gaps in shore jobs.

16   The Submarine Manning and Retention Review recommended the introduction of a £5,000 Golden Hello. This is now paid after basic training and completion of first sea draft. The Royal Navy have also put increased efforts into recruiting and raising the profile of submarine careers. These actions have paid off, as the numbers joining the Submarine Service have improved, and the number of non-volunteers has reduced significantly. Engineering remains one of the more difficult areas for recruiters, but the Royal Navy achieved 96 per cent of its targets for Ratings Engineers in 2005-06.

17   The length of time for recruits and trainees to become senior Nuclear Watchkeepers means that it is essential to retain as many as possible. Second Open Engagements of 10 years are offered to both Category A and Category B Nuclear Watchkeepers, and take up in 2005 was around 70 per cent. However, this does not guarantee a full 10 years service from everyone who signs up, as it is still possible to apply to leave early in this timeframe. The Royal Navy has offered a five year extension of service to those who do complete half of the Second Open Engagement, which would enable them to serve until age 55, although they would not be eligible for promotion. 10 out of 14 Warrant Officer 2s accepted this offer, and two out of 10 Chief Petty Officers.

18   In the longer term, the restructuring of the Engineering Branch should help to address some of the underlying problems in the branch. It is hoped the changes will be retention positive.

Removal from the operational pinch point register

19   Overall numbers of Nuclear Watchkeepers could recover by 2008-09. However, manning would still be imbalanced, with a 20 per cent deficit of Category A and Category B Watchkeepers and a surplus of Category C Watchkeepers. This will take longer to resolve, and it is therefore unlikely the trade would be removed from the pinch point register until 2014 at the earliest.

CASE STUDY TWO

Royal Navy Warfare Branch (General Service) Leading Hands

1 The Warfare Branch are the Royal Navy's seamanship specialists responsible for operating the communications, sensors and weapon systems in ships and submarines, gathering and co-ordinating information to help guide weapons to their targets and deflect enemy attacks, thus preventing damage to their own ship or submarine.

2 It takes several years to successfully complete all the training necessary to achieve the rank of Leading Hand in the Warfare Branch:

■ Phase 1 training – 8 weeks, to learn basic naval skills and discipline.

■ Phase 2 training builds on the skills learnt in phase 1 and individuals will be given specialist training in their chosen Warfare sub-specialisation (Warfare, Seaman, or Communications and Information Systems Specialist).

■ Recruits are classified as 'gain to trained strength' at the rank of Able Rate which costs around £42,000 per successful recruit to reach this point (2004-05 figures).

■ Individuals stay at Able Rate for approximately four to five years and are selected for promotion to Leading Hand where they will then be streamed into their particular branch of Warfare by the Branch Manager.

■ Phase 3 training consists of a number of targeted employment modules which seek to deliver specific and specialist skills as necessary.

Warfare Branch (General Service) manning

3 Shortfalls of Leading Hands over the last five years have increased from 13 per cent at 1 April 2001, to 30 per cent at 1 April 2005. At April 2006 there were 1,400 Leading Hands in the Warfare Branch, against a requirement of 1,770, representing a 21 per cent shortfall.

Why is this trade an operational pinch point?

4   The Leading Hand rank within the Warfare Branch is a pinch point due to past recruitment problems. In the early 1990s the Royal Navy was reducing in size and it was decided to cut recruitment to drive down numbers. This recruiting pause, from 1992 to 1996, created a 'black hole' which has moved through the ranks and is currently at the Leading Hand rank across the entire Royal Navy (paragraph 3.10, Volume 1).

5   The decreased Leading Hand population in the Warfare Branch is made worse by slow promotion from Able Rate to Leading Hand rank. This was in part due to the unwillingness of some Able Rates to go for promotion due to the increased workload at the Leading Hand rank, and delays in the lengthy promotion process.

6   There are currently no real problems recruiting people to the Warfare Branch, and recruitment targets have been exceeded in the last three years. Whilst the rate at which people are choosing to leave early is slightly higher than the target of five per cent for ratings, retention is not currently causing too much of a problem in the Warfare Branch.

Operational commitments

7   Operational commitments are always met, but ships are often deployed with a number of gapped posts. At present the under-manning at the Leading Hand rank is manageable as the more competent Able Rates, although not eligible for Leading Hand promotion, can perform the role of Leading Hand with the correct supervision from a Petty Officer. The manning shortfalls mean there are insufficient numbers of Leading Hands eligible for promotion to become Petty Officers. The Petty Officer is the main deliverer of operational capability and key supervisor on a ship.

Initiatives in place

8   A series of initiatives have been introduced to encourage faster promotion. The Warfare Branch Manager wrote to every Commanding Officer with a letter from the Chief of Staff to encourage them to get Able Rates to complete their task books and thus become eligible for promotion. There was a 40 per cent increase in the following three months in the numbers of Able Rates eligible for promotion. The career regulations have also been rewritten to reduce the delays in the promotion process.

9   Career structures within the Warfare Branch have been changed as part of the Navy Board Personnel Change Programme. Instead of spending a third of their time in each of the three specialisms (the operations room, the upper deck, maintenance of the weapons on board the ship) recruits will specialise in one chosen area. The necessary training can be completed in a shorter timeframe and thus recruits can be promoted as they will reach operational standard more quickly. There is an aim to change recruits expectations at entry to the Service, by emphasising the fact that progression is expected. This is hoped both to speed up promotion and to aid retention.

10   Even with these changes, modelling performed in June 2005 suggested that manning shortfalls may be as great as 58 per cent at the Petty Officer rank by 2014. The Royal Navy have therefore put in place further initiatives to restore structural sustainability.

11   There will be an annual check to ensure that the individual has the skills and capability to go on operations. If this 'operations' test is passed then the individual is automatically put forward for promotion. If a person fails they will be required to go on more training to improve their skills to the requisite level. Promotion will take only 12 months (from the point of being selected) rather than 18 months currently and there will be three promotion boards per year (in comparison to one at present). For new recruits there will be stricter requirements for the completion of task books.

12   There has been over-recruitment at Able Rate level in order to increase the pool from which to recruit Leading Hands. The over-manning at this level is also a reflection that a proportion of the Able Rates will already be performing Leading Hand roles.

13   The Royal Navy are planning to reduce the requirement for senior ratings in the long term by reviewing posts to establish if they still need to be filled by Petty Officers. The Royal Navy are keen to ensure that whilst some shore jobs will be civilianised, deleted, or transferred to different specialisations where there are not manning shortfalls, some shore jobs will be retained as 'respite' posts for the senior ranks when they return from deployments. At the same time the promotion to Chief Petty Officer may be slowed down. The whole process is likely to take several years to implement.

14   The Royal Navy has considered the possibility of sideways recruiting to Petty Officer rank. It was deemed unviable to recruit Petty Officers from other trades to the same rank in the Warfare Branch as the people would need to have the required training and experience which is built up over years. Instead, the Royal Navy are looking at a three year 'Fast Track Petty Officer' scheme. This will cover the same training as a normal Petty Officer, but in a much faster timescale, with individuals specifically assigned to train in 'opportunity-rich' ships. This is a small trial which commenced in May 2006 involving just six individuals. If this pilot scheme is deemed a success then up to 40 people could be fast tracked in the future.

Removal from the operational pinch point register

15   The Royal Navy expects that they will be living with the effect of the 'black hole' for at least the next ten years.

CASE STUDY THREE
Royal Marines Other Ranks (General Duties)

1 The Royal Marines are the Royal Navy's 'amphibious Infantry'. They are an elite Commando Force, able to deploy at short notice anywhere in the world to provide an amphibious assault force capability, or for rapid reaction intervention. They are capable of deployment in any terrain, and are specialists in mountain, jungle and cold weather environments.

2 Recruits are required to pass a two and a half day Potential Royal Marines Selection Course, before they can join the Royal Marines. They must complete 32 weeks of tough training, culminating in the Commando Course, a physically demanding set of tests of fitness, endurance and military professionalism, in order to earn the right to wear the 'green beret' of a Royal Marines Commando.

3 Most newly trained Marines join as Royal Marines (General Duties). Marines are also able to volunteer, or are selected for specialist training in one of 30 areas (for example Chef, Driver, Physical Training Instructor, Special Forces Operative).

4 It costs on average £79,600 to recruit and train a Royal Marine Other Rank (2004-05 figures) up to the point they become a gain to trained strength.

Royal Marine Other Ranks manning

5 The Royal Marines have been undermanned compared to the requirement for the last 10 years. Although the numbers of Royal Marines have increased in this period, an increasing requirement has meant that there is still a shortfall. At April 2006 there were 5,390 Royal Marine Other Ranks (General Duties), against a requirement of 5,960, which represents a 10 per cent deficit.

Why is this trade an operational pinch point?

6 The Royal Marines Other Ranks (General Duties) pinch point has arisen due to a combination of recruiting problems, higher than average rates of early exits, and an increase in the requirement for Royal Marines.

7 The Royal Navy did not meet its recruitment targets for Royal Marines Other Ranks in 2003-04, and 2004-05, due to a fall in the numbers of applicants **(Figure 2)**. The Royal Navy is not sure what caused this. It did coincide with a drop in marketing activity, and this may be a contributory factor. Equally it may be due to circumstances outside the Royal Navy's control. Actions taken by the Royal Navy have meant that recruiting performance improved markedly in 2005-06, but an increase in the requirement[2] means that there was still a recruiting shortfall. It will take time for the increased numbers to reach the trained strength.

8 The impact of the Royal Navy's 'black hole', caused by cutbacks in recruiting, can be seen in the deficits at Corporal and Sergeant ranks. As Marines are promoted, these deficits should improve, but the deficit at the lowest rank, Marine, will increase in the short-term, particularly as the recruiting problems between 2003 and 2005 mean insufficient numbers coming out of training to replace the promotees. In addition, there are signs that due to the rate and point at which personnel at Marine Rank apply to leave early, there may be difficulty in meeting the promotion numbers due to the lack of experience in the pool of Marines available for pull-through to Corporal then to Sergeant. This has the potential to prolong recovery at these ranks.

9 The voluntary outflow rate has exceeded the Royal Navy's five per cent guideline rate in every year since 2001, and is above average for the Royal Navy as a whole **(Figure 3)**. Voluntary outflow, which has been increasing since 2003, is forecast to remain high, particularly as the 2005-06 voluntary outflow application rate was at its highest since 1997 (8.5 per cent at the end of 2005-06).

10 Evidence from our survey of pinch point trades, and the retention study carried out by the Royal Marines Working Group set up to look at recruitment and retention, indicates that as well as the general concerns shared by all the trades surveyed (inability to plan life outside work, impact of Service life on family life, attractions of civilian employment), Royal Marines are particularly dissatisfied with pay and allowances, and that this is influencing some decisions to leave early.

11 The requirement for Marines has been growing since 1997, with the increase in land oriented joint operations, and continues to do so. This takes place against a background of overall reductions in the strength of the Royal Navy but an increase in the Royal Navy's commitment to amphibious capability. Royal Marines manning is, in effect, chasing a moving target, as it is difficult to upsize in strength at the same pace as the requirement increases.

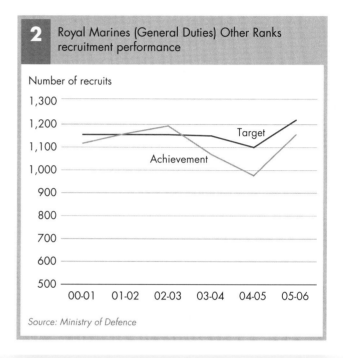

2 Royal Marines (General Duties) Other Ranks recruitment performance

Source: Ministry of Defence

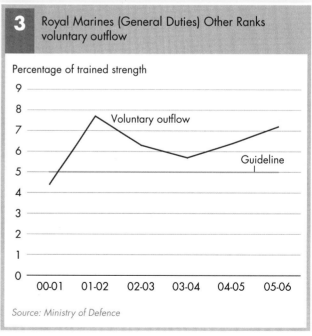

3 Royal Marines (General Duties) Other Ranks voluntary outflow

Source: Ministry of Defence

2 The increase in requirement has been in the region of 6.5 per cent over the last six years and follows directly from the demand for the Royal Marines contributions to the three main growth areas of Defence, namely Amphibious Capability, Special Forces and Joint Commitments.

Operational commitments

12 Operational tempo is not the main problem for the Royal Marines. Harmony guidelines, as with the rest of the Royal Navy, are not being exceeded, except by small numbers of people in a few specialist areas. Royal Marines who responded to our survey viewed deployments more positively than other groups. Operational tempo needs to be at a certain level to keep Royal Marines interested and to maintain their experience.

13 The gapping of posts, caused by the manpower shortages, is more of a problem. Certain units in the Royal Marines need to be at or near full manning to meet are operational readiness states. None of the units are below 70 per cent manning deployable strength. However, two units are in the low to mid-70 per cent range in terms of deployable strength and mid-70 per cent to 80 per cent range in terms of manning states. This can mean that individuals may be moved around more, in order to fill posts in the priority areas.

Initiatives in place

14 A Working Group was set up in 2004 to tackle the problems in the Royal Marine trade.

15 Improving recruitment, and ensuring that the training system is at full capacity over the next few years are seen by the Royal Navy as key in bringing the Royal Marines back to full manning. The Royal Navy allocated an extra £3.3 million for Royal Marine marketing and other recruiting initiatives in 2005-06, including:

■ increased television and cinema advertising;

■ increased presence in Armed Forces Careers Offices and extra personnel to help with the recruiting effort, including a Royal Marines Corps Colonel;

■ Commando Display Teams and Sports Presentation Teams promoting the Royal Marines; and

■ Meet the Marines courses – aimed at potential recruits, and offering them the opportunity to learn more about life as a Marine.

16 The impact can be seen in the improved recruitment performance in 2005-06. Enquiries were up 26 per cent compared to 2004-05, applications to join increased by 22 per cent, and numbers recruited by 18 per cent. Additional funding for television and cinema advertising is no longer available, and the Meet the Marines events have now been completed.

17 Financial incentives had some success in bringing in additional manpower:

■ Recruiting Bounty: £1,000 offered to those who recruit a friend who completes 15 weeks training (most who reach this stage will go on to complete the full course). A total of 84 have been paid, as well as four bonuses of £500, at a total cost of £86,000.

■ Re-join Bounties:

  ■ £6,000 for fully trained Marines – 39 paid in 2005-06, total cost £234,000.

  ■ £1-3,000 for partly trained Marines – six paid in 2005-06, total cost £10,000.

18 Improving pass rates was also seen as a key way to improve the numbers joining. The high standards required to pass Royal Marines training means that a large number of recruits are lost in training (training wastage is over 40 per cent). A combination of initiatives, including a higher instructor-to-recruit ratio, counselling and mentoring, has improved the pass rate to 57 per cent, which the Royal Marines are now aiming to maintain. The pass rate for the Potential Royal Marines Course has also improved.

19 The Working Group has also been looking at retention, with a view to reducing the current high rate of early exits. They are reviewing areas such as the timing of commitment bonus payments, and some of the non-financial issues, for example looking at ways to slow down 'drafting churn' so that individuals can stay with one unit for longer periods of time, developing better mechanisms for giving notice for tasks, and improving the career management system. In the long-term, strategic work on areas of manpower development will feed into the wider Navy Board Personnel Change Programme.

Removal from the operational pinch point register

20 In theory, manning balance could be achieved by 2010-11, if the Royal Navy consistently achieves recruitment targets for Royal Marines and maintains the higher pass rates in training. If the Royal Navy achieves only 85 per cent of its recruitment targets, returning to manning balance may be delayed until 2020. In practice, the Royal Navy currently expects to achieve around 90-95 per cent of the targets. The high rate of early exits remains a concern, and is another factor likely to delay recovery to manning balance. If voluntary outflow rates can be reduced, the Royal Navy should be able to recover the shortfalls more quickly.

CASE STUDY FOUR
Army Recovery Mechanic (Royal Electrical and Mechanical Engineers)

1 A Recovery Mechanic's role is the extraction of a vehicle or piece of equipment from where it has become immobile or ineffective and rectifying or removing that equipment to where it can be repaired. The role of the Recovery Mechanic requires a diverse skill set which includes: driving heavy vehicles, route planning, dealing with mines and booby traps, diving and recovery skills.

2 Training to be a Recovery Mechanic is relatively short in terms of theory based teaching and is therefore heavily dependent on experience gained in the field.

- Phase 1 training – 12 weeks. Completed by all soldier recruits.

- Phase 2 training – 175 days to become a Craftsman/Class 3 Recovery Mechanic. A Class 3 Craftsman can work under direct supervision to get on-the-job training.

- To recruit and train up to this point, when the soldier is classified as a 'gain to the trained strength' costs approximately £54,000 for each successful individual (2004-05 figures).

- Class 2 training – 28 day course builds on the experience gained in the field. This is completed after approximately six months as a Class 3 craftsman. Class 2 Recovery Mechanics (Lance Corporal) can work under minimum supervision.

- Class 1 training – 35.5 days. Normally attended by personnel who have been at Class 2 for approximately four years. On completion of the Class 1 course, personnel take on a supervisory role at Corporal rank.

Recovery Mechanic manning

3   As at April 2006 the requirement for Recovery Mechanics was 595, at the same date the strength of the trade was 485, thus there was an overall manning shortfall of 18.5 per cent. The trade has experienced similar shortfalls for the past five years. The under-manning is however most prevalent at the ranks of Lance Corporal-Class 2 (26 per cent under-manning at October 2005) and Corporal-Class 1 (53 per cent under-manning).

Why is this trade an operational pinch point?

4   The reason the Recovery Mechanic trade is a pinch point is threefold: past recruitment problems, increased requirement and a difficult trade structure to manage.

5   During the mid-1990s there was a perception that the Army was not recruiting which was driven by the publicity generated by 'Options for Change' and which saw a significant reduction in the size of the Armed Forces. Whilst the Army continued to recruit during this period, it witnessed a significant downturn in recruiting performance from 1992-94. By 1999 recruitment in the Recovery Mechanic trade was improving, but there was also an increase in the requirement.

6   The role of the Recovery Mechanic impacts on the structure required for the trade. The most experienced Recovery Mechanics (Class 1/Corporal and Class 2/Lance Corporal) are most in demand; these individuals are needed in all roles as they are the only ones able to work in the front line and are also needed to supervise Class 3 Craftsmen back on base doing third line repairs.

7   Recruiting has improved significantly over the past few years and the Army has successfully recruited 100 per cent of its target in the past two years **(Figure 4)**. In 2005-06, 113 personnel were recruited against a target of 109. However there are not enough Craftsmen to feed up to Lance Corporal and Corporal ranks.

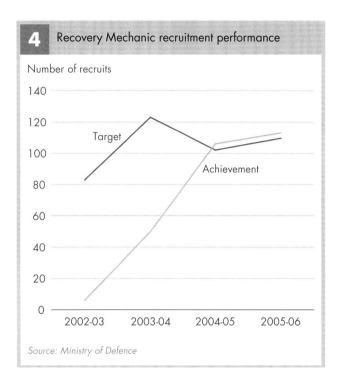

4 Recovery Mechanic recruitment performance

Source: Ministry of Defence

8   Retention has been less of a problem in the Recovery Mechanic trade; the percentage of people choosing to leave early is approximately 4.5 per cent, which is below the Army average. Retention is, however, still a concern within this trade as it is important that personnel are retained beyond the six to eight year point in order that there are sufficient numbers with Class 1 experience. There are concerns that the number of people choosing to leave early has increased in recent years, but it is too early to say whether this is the beginning of a longer-term trend.

Operational commitments

9   The level of commitments has increased in the past few years, and is likely to remain high in 2006 and 2007 given ongoing commitments in Iraq and Afghanistan.

10 Despite the manning shortfalls, commitments are being met. However, harmony guidelines are being broken by many personnel in order to meet all commitments. The effect of shortages is that individuals with Class 1 or 2 qualifications are deployed more frequently, with shorter gaps between deployments. The increased levels of separation may cause added pressure on the individual's family life and ability to plan their own life. In the 30 month period to 31 December 2005, 34.5 per cent of Recovery Mechanics were breaking individual harmony guidelines. The bulk of the separated service is time spent away on operations, given that the training courses are relatively short.

11 Personnel qualified to Class 1 and 2 are responsible for supervising the less experienced Class 3 personnel. Operational posts are filled as a necessity, which leaves some non-operational posts gapped, for example there are fewer Class 1 personnel to fill a supervisory role for the Craftsmen.

Initiatives in place

12 As an operational pinch point, the Recovery Mechanic trade is the focus of continued efforts by the recruitment staff who have been tasked with meeting operational pinch point recruitment targets.

13 The Recovery Mechanic trade participate in the Satisfied Soldier Scheme. This is a scheme whereby trainee soldiers may be sent to work in recruitment offices, or into local schools and colleges to talk about their experiences.

14 The Recovery Mechanic training is now accredited with City and Guilds qualification to encourage potential recruits.

15 A number of financial incentives are offered to increase recruitment into the trade:

■ Golden Hello – £500 for each recruit with basic entry standard qualifications. Ninety five awarded at a cost of £49,500 (one individual received a Golden Hello of £2,500).

■ Eight Transfer Bonuses of £1,500 each have been paid and one is being processed.

■ One Re-join Bounty of £6,000 has been paid.

16 In order to fill the manning shortfalls at the higher ranks, Phase 2 training output has been increased to over-man at the Craftsman level; however this will take time to feed upwards to the higher ranks. The Army is trying to push people through training more quickly and is putting people in for the exams up to six months earlier than in the past. The age criteria for promotion from Corporal to Sergeant have also been removed to enable faster promotion.

Removal from the operational pinch point register

17 The Army currently anticipate that the Recovery Mechanic trade will be removed from the operational pinch point register in 2008-09. This timescale is largely dependent on early exits remaining low, achieving recruiting and input targets, and the demand for Recovery Mechanics not being further increased. However, even when the trade group falls within overall manning balance there will still remain gaps at certain ranks.

CASE STUDY FIVE
Army Ammunition Technician (Royal Logistic Corps)

1   Ammunition Technicians are the Army's experts in conventional bomb disposal, chemical, biological, radiological munitions disposal, and improvised explosive device disposal. They play a vital role in delivering the operational capability of the Army in peace and on operations by ensuring that the Army's stock of ammunition is stored, transported and used correctly and safely. The Ammunition Technician trade is responsible for improvised explosive device disposal, more commonly known as 'counter terrorist bomb disposal'. Ammunition Technicians are trained and equipped to deal with all types of improvised explosive device that might be encountered and are prepared for immediate deployment at any time of the day or night in response to potential threats both on the battlefield and in peacetime.

2   Training to become an Ammunition Technician:

■   Phase 1 training – 12 weeks. Completed by all soldier recruits.

■   Phase 2 training – 39 weeks – to become a 'Class 2' or 'No 2'.

■   To recruit and train up to this point, when the soldier is classified as a 'gain to trained strength' costs approximately £60,500 for each successful individual (2005-06 figures). An individual cannot be deployed until completion of the Joint Service Level course.

■   Joint Service Level (Low Threat) Course - five weeks. Completion of the course enables deployment in a low threat environment, for example Great Britain.

■   High Threat Course – six weeks to enable deployment overseas.

■   Class 1 training – 20 week course builds on the experience gained in the field. This is completed after approximately two years (12 months spent in the Field Army, 12 months spent in the ammunition depot).

3   Ammunition Technicians need to do regular training to keep their skills, knowledge and qualifications up to date. Improvised explosive devices, especially, are constantly changing and are becoming increasingly sophisticated. As such it is necessary for Ammunition Technicians to undertake strict re-licensing every six months.

Ammunition Technician manning

4   As at April 2006 the requirement for Ammunition Technicians was 367, at the same date the strength was 275, thus there was an overall manning shortfall of 25 per cent. Similar shortfalls have existed for the last five years. The manning shortfalls are, however, most prevalent at the ranks of Corporal 'Class 2' (45 per cent shortfall as at October 2005) and Sergeant 'Class 1' (47 per cent shortfall) which are the key deliverers of operational capability.

Why is this trade an operational pinch point?

5   There was a formal decision to stop recruitment into the Ammunition Technician trade for the two years 1997-98 to 1998-99 as a cost saving measure. This meant 36 people did not join during these two years (out of a trade group with strength of 275). This pause in recruitment has contributed to the current manning shortfalls within the trade, which has moved through the rank structure and is currently at the rank of Sergeant.

6   Ammunition Technician training is one of the lengthiest and most demanding within the Army. This is necessary for the safety of personnel carrying out complex and dangerous tasks in often hazardous environments. There is a high failure rate on the courses with approximately 40-60 per cent success rate on the Joint Service Level course and as low as 30-40 per cent success rate for the High Threat Course on the first attempt. Entrants now require a GCSE Grade C as a minimum which should improve the standard of recruits but has the effect of limiting the pool from which to recruit.

7   Ammunition Technicians voluntary outflow rate is below the Army guideline **(Figure 5)**, and the trade has one of the longest return of services (average length of career is 19.1 years, the Army average is 9.6 years). The Department attributes this in part to the fact that there are few civilian equivalent jobs. However, there are concerns that the number of people choosing to leave early has shown an upward trend in recent years, but it is too early to say whether this is the beginning of a longer-term trend.

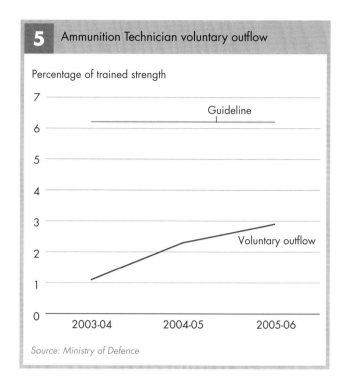

5   Ammunition Technician voluntary outflow

Percentage of trained strength

Source: Ministry of Defence

Operational commitments

8   The heightened terrorist threat in recent years has meant that Ammunition Technicians have had greater commitments on the domestic front as well as being heavily deployed on overseas operations. The level of commitments overseas has increased in the past few years, and is likely to remain high in 2006 and 2007. As at November 2005, 48.5 per cent of Ammunition Technicians were deployed on operations.

9   Despite the manning shortfalls, commitments are being met. However, harmony guidelines are being broken by many personnel in order to meet all commitments. In the 30 month period to December 2005, 21.1 per cent of Ammunition Technicians were breaking individual harmony guidelines.

10   Seventy eight per cent of Ammunition Technicians in the Army are within 11 EOD Regiment. 11 EOD Regiment has a requirement of 206 but a strength of only 121 (as at November 2005), of which not all are fully deployable (not fully qualified, those preparing to go on operations, those on post-operation tour leave). Within the Regiment, 80 out of 121 are on duty with three hours 'notice to move' or less, either within Great Britain or overseas. Many Ammunition Technicians on duty in Great Britain will still be unable to return home in the evening as being on three hours 'notice to move' will require individuals to stay in barracks so they can respond immediately if a situation should arise.

11 One impact of the shortages of personnel, combined with the ever increasing demands, is that some jobs which used to be ring-fenced, for example at the School of Ammunition and the Army Training and Recruitment Agency, are no longer protected. Some instructors are now being asked to do other tasks and go on operations. There is a risk that this will have an impact on the number of courses being run and the amount of training being offered.

Initiatives in place

12 As an operational pinch point the Ammunition Technician trade has been the focus of increased recruitment effort. An Ammunition Technician Sergeant has been tasked as a dedicated specialist recruiter to raise awareness of the trade and increase recruitment.

13 The Army introduced an Ammunition Technician Careers Advisory Board in August 2005, which aims to pre-select those recruits who are likely to pass the difficult exams and thus reduce wastage on the courses. It is too early to assess the success of this initiative.

14 A number of financial incentives have been introduced to try and increase recruitment into the trade. These have been offered with mixed success:

- Golden Hellos – £500 to those with basic entry standards, £2,500 to those with A levels. To date 149 awarded at a total cost of £94,500.

- Transfer bonus – £1,500, taken up by 15 individuals.

- Rejoin bounties – £6,000, no takers.

- Bursaries – £1,500, no takers.

15 Recruiting performance in the trade has improved significantly in the past couple of years due to the increased focus the trade receives as an operational pinch point (**Figure 6**).

16 However, given the long training time it will take a number of years before the new recruits feed through to the trained strength. In the meantime the Army has introduced a number of measures to deal with the current manning shortfalls.

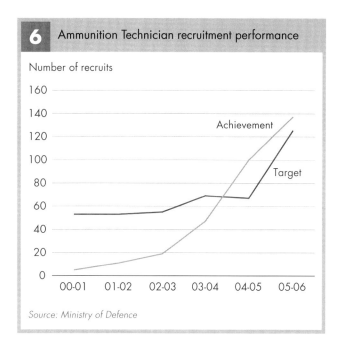

6 Ammunition Technician recruitment performance

Number of recruits

Source: Ministry of Defence

17 In an attempt to increase the frequency with which Ammunition Technicians can be deployed, four month tours are being trialled within the trade. With four month deployments, mid- and post- tour leave can be reduced and the individual can therefore be deployed again sooner.

18 There are currently a small number of individuals who have been offered extended service for a period of two years, known as continuance. A Long Service Scheme will replace continuance from next year with a view to extending an individual's length of service by five years. There are plans to have approximately eight to 10 individuals on the Long Service Scheme each year.

Removal from the operational pinch point register

19 The Ammunition Technician trade is predicted to be fully manned by January 2008; but this is largely dependent on meeting the current ambitious targets for getting 80 per cent through training, early exit rates remaining low, and the Army achieving its recruitment targets. However, even when the trade group falls within overall manning balance there will remain gaps at certain ranks.

CASE STUDY SIX
Army Information Systems Engineer (Royal Signals)

1 Information Systems Engineers are military communications and IT specialists, responsible for the management of the Information Systems in the battlefield environment and elsewhere. Demand for this capability has increased with the growing importance of data and information management and the growth of more complex battle space and IT technology (including Battlefield Digitisation and Network Enabled Capability).

2 The Information Systems Engineer trade has only existed since April 2004, the first direct entry recruits joined in July 2004, and the first Class 1 course was run in January 2005. The trade was previously known as Information Systems Operator and Supervisor Information Systems and the first training courses were introduced in 2000. This trade was filled by experienced personnel transferring from within the Royal Signals.

3 Information Systems Engineer is a technical trade. It takes several years to successfully complete all the training and reach supervisor level:

- Phase 1 training – 12 weeks.

- Phase 2 trade training – 19 week course to become a Class 3 Information Systems Engineer. To recruit and train to this point, when the soldier is counted as a gain to trained strength, costs approximately £39,000 for each individual (2005-06 figures).

- Class 2 training in Unit for approximately two years. Entrance exam.

- Phase 3 trade training – 20 week course to become a Class 1 Information Systems Engineer, Sergeant rank.

- Recommendation for selection for Supervisor training, and promotion to Staff Sergeant. 31 week Supervisor training course.

4   Information Systems Engineers also need to do regular training to keep their skills, qualifications and knowledge up to date, as IT systems change constantly, and in some instances they may be required to work on non-standard IT systems.

Information Systems Engineer manning

5   Information Systems Engineer has been included on the operational pinch point register since this document was created in 2003. At April 2006 there were 301 Information Systems Engineers against a requirement of 378, which represents a 20 per cent shortfall. The main deficits are at the ranks of Sergeant (99 against a requirement of 115, 14 per cent shortfall), Corporal (95 against a requirement of 138, 31 per cent shortfall), and Signaller (37 against a requirement of 65, 43 per cent shortfall).

Why is this trade an operational pinch point?

6   Prior to 2004 the trade was fed by individuals from other trades in the Royal Signals and elsewhere, who were often at the later stages of their careers. The trade had no Signallers or Lance Corporals prior to 2003, and this has contributed to today's shortfalls at Sergeant and Corporal ranks. This means that the trade has an older age

profile, with some experienced personnel due to leave within the next three years, without sufficient numbers coming through to replace them. It will take time for those recruited directly since 2004 to reach those ranks at which there are the biggest shortfalls.

7   There were some problems recruiting to the trade in the first year. The Army recruitment computer system was not showing the qualifications required for the Royal Signals correctly, and this may have been a contributory factor. In 2005-06, the Army recruited 41 against a target of 51. Recruitment remains challenging as the higher academic and Army Selection Standards and the demands of the technical training for this trade limit the potential recruit pool.

8   The requirement for Information Systems Engineers has increased, and continues to do so. This means that despite improvements in numbers since 2002, full manning has not yet been achieved (**Figure 7**). The requirement is set to increase by a further 97 to 475 by April 2008.

9   Some units may require Information Systems Engineers before they have formally established an Information Systems Engineer post, therefore there may be some 'augmentee' posts which are not yet counted in the requirements. The Royal Signals also have to fill their allocation (124 posts as at November 2005) of the Army's 'E2' posts. These are general roles, which

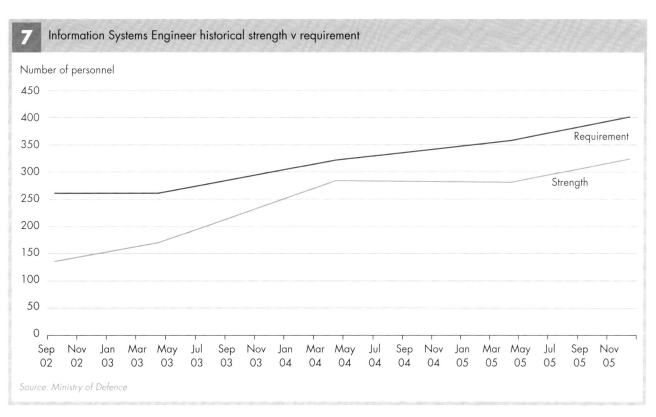

7 Information Systems Engineer historical strength v requirement

Number of personnel

Source: Ministry of Defence

do not necessarily have to be filled by someone from a specific trade. The posts can exist for up to three years, and the need to fill these roles adds to the demands on the Information Systems Engineer trade and can lead to gapped posts in other areas. The number of these posts is also forecast to increase by 2008.

10 Retention has been a problem in the past for the Royal Signals, whose personnel are attractive to civilian employers due to their skills and qualifications. A financial retention incentive was introduced for some trades in an attempt to reduce the numbers leaving for highly paid jobs in the telecommunications industry (Appendix Three, Volume 1). Information Systems Engineers voluntary outflow rate was one per cent in 2003-04, 2.7 per cent in 2004-05, and 3.1 per cent in 2005-06.

Operational commitments

11 The level of commitments has increased, and is likely to remain high in 2006 given ongoing commitments in Iraq and Afghanistan. Information Systems and IT support are crucial for all operations. As at November 2005, 24 per cent of Information Systems Engineers were deployed on operations. Demands from United Kingdom operations have also grown with recent commitments such as support for counter-terrorism requiring increasingly sophisticated information and communications systems.

12 Despite the manning shortfalls, commitments are being met. However, harmony guidelines are being broken by many personnel in order to meet all commitments, and personnel are being moved around between Units to fill priority posts.

13 United Kingdom operations are mainly high-readiness tasks, and the impact of manning shortfalls means that some individuals can spend every other month on the highest states of readiness, with the short 'notice to move' periods affecting their ability to plan outside work. Some personnel (11 Signal Brigade) are spending on average 24 months out of 30 months either on operations, exercise, or on high-readiness.

14 Personnel from better manned trades within the Royal Signals are being used, after receiving relevant training, to fill some Information Systems Engineer roles on operations. These personnel are required to be supervised by a Class 2 Information Systems Engineer, so this can add to the pressures on supervisors.

Initiatives in place

15 As an operational pinch point trade, Information Systems Engineer is noted on the job briefs of recruiters and is a focus of continued efforts to meet operational pinch point recruitment targets.

16 The Royal Signals routinely interview recruits at Phase 1 training, when it is possible to reallocate trades for recruits before trade training begins. The Royal Signals also use the Army Transfer Fairs to recruit those looking to change trades. Transfers from within the Royal Signals are another source of recruits, particularly as the Royal Signals have one trade, Systems Engineering Technician, which had a 26 per cent surplus as at December 2005.

17 Financial retention incentives were offered in the Royal Signals on completion of various courses, and the predecessor trade to Information Systems Engineer was one of those that qualified (Appendix Three, Volume 1) The financial retention incentives played a role in improving retention and early exit rates; however, they were withdrawn in 2004 due to budget cuts.

18 It will take time for those individuals recruited direct to the trade to reach the areas of shortage at more senior ranks. In the meantime, posts are prioritised to ensure that the most important are filled and manpower from other sources used to reduce some of the demands on Information Systems Engineers. As well as using personnel with transferable skills from their better manned trades to fill some Information Systems Engineer posts on operations, similar redistribution can be used to fill some of the more general 'E2' roles, particularly from the Systems Engineering Technician trade which is in surplus. Approximately 15 posts are filled by senior Non-Commissioned Officers and Warrant Officers on two to three year 'continuance' contracts.

Removal from the operational pinch point register

19 The Army currently anticipates that Information Systems Engineer will be fully manned, and therefore can be removed from the operational pinch point register in 2007-08. This is dependent on early exits remaining low, achieving recruiting and input targets, and the liability and demands for Information Systems Engineer posts not being further increased.

CASE STUDY SEVEN
Army Explosive Ordnance Disposal (Royal Engineers)

1 Explosive Ordnance Disposal are the Royal Engineers' bomb disposal experts. They are responsible for the location, identification and safe disposal of unexploded ordnance (shells, bombs and other munitions, including chemical and biological) both in a battlefield environment, and in peacetime. This includes disposal of unexploded World War Two bombs in the United Kingdom. They are also experts in counter terrorist search, uncovering stores of illegal arms and explosives, and specialist search for munitions secreted by hostile forces. Explosive Ordnance Disposal personnel do not deal with improvised explosive devices.

2 Recruits do not join the Explosive Ordnance Disposal specialisation directly. Royal Engineers can choose to specialise in Explosive Ordnance Disposal after their common training:

- 12 week basic military training as a soldier.

- 10 week Combat Engineer training to acquire military engineering skills.

- Tradesman training – length depends on which of the 18 trades the recruit chooses to specialise in, each leads to recognised civilian qualifications.

- Possible to choose to become a Specialist Engineer. Those who choose to specialise in Bomb Disposal join 33 Engineer Regiment (EOD).

- Two week elementary course, followed by a period of experience, promotion, and four week intermediate course.

- Officers and senior Non-Commissioned Officers can do a seven week advanced course to become Bomb Disposal Officers. Soldiers do not usually serve as a Bomb Disposal Officer for their whole career, but will alternate postings with other Units.

Information on recruiting and training costs is not available for this specialisation.

Explosive Ordnance Disposal manning

3   The numbers of Explosive Ordnance Disposal personnel have increased from 510 at 1 April 2004 to 558 at 1 April 2006. However, the increase in requirement from 592 personnel at 1 April 2005 to 644 personnel at 1 April 2006 means that there is still a shortfall of 13 per cent. This is not evenly distributed across the rank structure.

Why is this trade an operational pinch point?

4   The Explosive Ordnance Disposal pinch point has arisen as the demands for this specialisation have increased, without an equivalent increase in manning strength. The requirement for Explosive Ordnance Disposal increased in 2006, and it will take time to grow the manpower to meet the new requirement. The level of commitments, with tasks both at home and overseas means that the current limited resource is over-tasked. In November 2005 42 per cent of Explosive Ordnance Disposal were on operations or deployments throughout the world.

5   Explosive Ordnance Disposal is a specialisation within the Royal Engineers, which soldiers can join after completing their trade training, therefore there are no direct entry recruits. For the Royal Engineers as a whole, meeting higher recruiting targets which come with the increased requirement under Future Army Structures is not seen as a problem, as competition to join is usually high.

6   The Department does not hold separate voluntary outflow data for the Explosive Ordnance Disposal trade. Voluntary outflow rates for the Royal Engineers as a whole have traditionally been high and at April 2006 were running two per cent above the Army guideline. The Royal Engineers have seen a recent increase in voluntary outflow, but it is too early to say whether this is the beginning of a longer-term trend.

Operational commitments

7   13.9 per cent of Explosive Ordnance Disposal personnel (which includes all Royal Engineer personnel serving with an Explosive Ordnance Disposal Unit) were breaching the Army's individual harmony guidelines in the 30 months to December 2005. Commitments have remained high in 2006 with deployments to Afghanistan adding to existing commitments overseas and support for counter terrorism activities in the United Kingdom.

Initiatives in place

8   In total, the requirement for Explosive Ordnance Disposal will increase by 25 per cent under Future Army Structures, as under the current structure the specialisation is too small for all the demands placed on it. 33 Engineer Regiment (EOD) will get an additional sixth squadron (17 Field Squadron). The Royal Engineers anticipate that the new squadron, included in the requirement from 1 April 2006, should be 90 per cent manned by October 2007. This can partly be done by transferring people from elsewhere within the Royal Engineers to this capability. In addition, efforts are currently going into recruiting for the Royal Engineers in order to meet all the increased requirements in place by 2008. Recruiting to full strength will take some time, partly as the training capacity limits the numbers who can be recruited each year.

9   Gapped posts arising from manning shortages are being carefully managed during the transition to Future Army Structures, in order to ensure the highest priority posts are manned. Restrictions on offering two to three year 'continuance' contracts have been lifted in the Royal Engineers, as have restrictions on offering Full Time Reserve Service contracts. It is hoped this will help to fill some of the gapped posts.

10   There is early work underway looking at improving retention, as full manning will be achieved sooner if the rate of early exits is reduced. This includes reviewing some of the 'non-financial' retention factors, such as meeting personal preferences in drafting.

Removal from the operational pinch point register

11   The Army currently anticipates that Explosive Ordnance Disposal will be removed from the pinch point register in 2008-09. For the Royal Engineers as a whole, full manning to the increased requirements will only be achieved by 2012 if voluntary outflow rates fall closer to the Army average. If they remain at the current rate of 8.2 per cent achieving this target will take longer.

CASE STUDY EIGHT
Royal Air Force Weapons System Operators (Linguists)

1   The role of a Weapons System Operator (Linguist) is to provide linguist capability on an airborne platform – the Nimrod R1. This is a small and specialist trade whose role is to interpret signal traffic both on a tactical and strategic basis.

2   It takes several years to successfully complete all the training necessary to be a Linguist:

■   Phase 1 training – nine weeks. Common to all Royal Air Force recruits.

■   Non-Commissioned Aircrew initial training – 36 weeks.

■   Intensive language training courses – 12 to 18 months.

■   Applied language training course – six months – understanding how to apply linguistic skills in a military context.

■   Nimrod R1 equipment training course – four months.

■   Recruit is now classified as 'Into Productive Service' which costs £118,000 per successful recruit (2004-05 figures).

■   Combat skills course – nine months. On completion of the course the recruit will be deemed 'Combat Ready' and is thus deployable.

3   Linguists are required to do regular training to maintain their language capability in at least two languages, and must learn new languages as necessary to meet operational requirements.

4   Given the length and cost of training, each recruit is required to sign up for a six year initial return of service, plus an additional three years for each subsequent language acquired.

Linguist manning

5   As at April 2006 the requirement for Linguists was 70 and the strength at the same date was 35, thus there was an overall manning shortfall of 50 per cent. Linguists have had manning shortfalls ranging from 33 per cent to 50 per cent in each of the past five years.

Why is this trade an operational pinch point?

6   Historically recruitment has been a problem, even though the target number of recruits is only 10 per year. The Royal Air Force has recruited from the public domain only in the last three to five years, as previously 90 per cent of recruits to the Linguist trade were internal transfers from the ground trades. Since then the Royal Air Force has had difficulties recruiting due to the lengthy and difficult training commitment, difficulties attracting the necessary calibre of recruit with language qualifications or with excellent linguistic abilities, many of whom are lost to university and to translator roles in civilian employment. The Royal Air Force is also competing with the Army due to greater public awareness of Army Linguist roles. Although recruitment targets for this specialisation have been achieved for the last two years, the lengthy training requirement means the manning situation is unlikely to improve for a few years.

7   Retention of Linguists is extremely important, especially given the time taken to recruit and train a replacement individual to an equivalent level. The guideline target for voluntary outflow is 2.5 per cent of the trade strength (**Figure 8**). This has been exceeded in the Linguist trade since 1998-99. The percentages below represent only small numbers of individuals, however even one or two individuals leaving can have a large impact on the trade given its small overall size.

Operational commitments

8   Despite serious manning shortfalls, operational commitments are always met but this is largely due to operators' readiness to spend long periods out of the country and to work long hours, potentially shifts of up to 12 hours. This is difficult work given the high levels of concentration needed. The effect of shortages is that Linguists are deployed more frequently, with shorter gaps between deployments. The increased levels of separation, and often short notice given for operations, may cause added pressure on the individual's family life and ability to plan their own life.

9   Harmony guidelines setting out recommended tour intervals, and targets on separated service are routinely being broken by Linguists in order to meet the operational commitments (**Figure 9**).

10   The requirement for each Linguist to maintain expertise in at least two languages through ongoing training further depletes numbers available for deployments. There are risks that the high level of operational commitments could mean there is less time to go on language refresher courses and professional courses and capability may be affected.

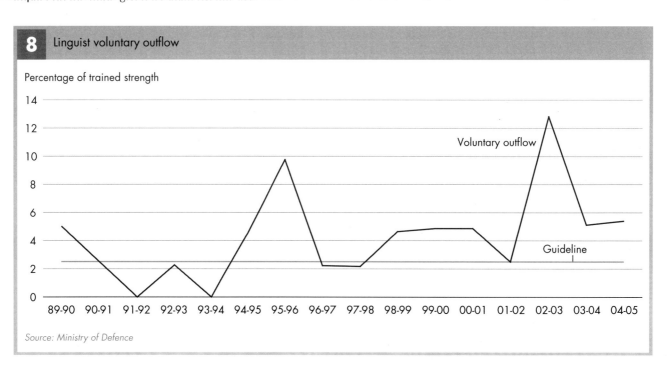

8   Linguist voluntary outflow

Percentage of trained strength

Source: Ministry of Defence

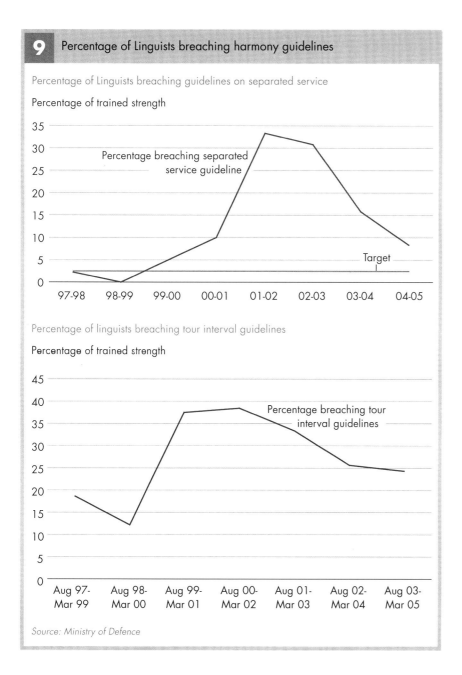

9 Percentage of Linguists breaching harmony guidelines

Percentage of Linguists breaching guidelines on separated service

Percentage of trained strength

Percentage breaching separated service guideline

Target

97-98 98-99 99-00 00-01 01-02 02-03 03-04 04-05

Percentage of linguists breaching tour interval guidelines

Percentage of trained strength

Percentage breaching tour interval guidelines

Aug 97-Mar 99 Aug 98-Mar 00 Aug 99-Mar 01 Aug 00-Mar 02 Aug 01-Mar 03 Aug 02-Mar 04 Aug 03-Mar 05

Source: Ministry of Defence

Initiatives in place

11   The Non-Commissioned Aircrew liaison team was created in October 2003 to improve recruitment into all Non-Commissioned Aircrew specialisations, particularly to the Linguist trade. The Non-Commissioned Aircrew liaison team is a three man team, including one Linguist. They visit schools, career fairs, and language universities to promote the Non-Commissioned Aircrew cadre. The team was introduced as a two and a half year scheme, due to finish in March 2006. Due to the success of the team in meeting recruitment targets it has been decided to continue with this initiative until March 2008. In 2005-06 the Non-Commissioned Aircrew liaison team contributed to the achievement of 100 per cent of the recruitment target for the Linguist trade.

12   In 2002 the Royal Air Force commissioned the Airman Aircrew Sustainability Study; a 10 year strategic plan, to ensure long-term sustainability of the Non-Commissioned Aircrew cadre. This review recommended the introduction of a financial retention incentive to improve retention across the entire cadre. A payment of up to £20,000 is awarded to all Non-Commissioned Aircrew who have completed 17 years service or more, in return for a five year return of service, or service to the 22 year point, whichever is the earliest. The Scheme ended on 31 March 2006, after a three year period. As at December 2005, 19 Linguists had taken this up at a total cost of £336,500.

13   The Airman Aircrew Sustainability Study also recommended the introduction of the Professional Aviator Spine, an alternative career structure which provides enhanced rates of pay to experienced personnel in order to retain them for a full career until age 55. Currently 10 Linguists are on the Professional Aviator Spine and a further two have been made an offer and have accepted.

14   There have also been changes in the way the Non-Commissioned Aircrew cadre are trained. Previously Linguists were trained separately to other Non-Commissioned Aircrew. Now, the system is more modular, which makes it easier to move people between specialisations. This allows internal recruitment to the Linguist trade, for example some Weapons System Operators (Air Engineering) are retraining to become Linguists. In the future, when the Linguist trade is at full strength it is hoped that individuals will be able to have a more varied role by gaining experience in other Weapon System Operator roles for short periods. This is hoped to aid retention.

Removal from the operational pinch point register

15   The Royal Air Force currently anticipates that the trade will be in manning balance by 2010. However, this is dependent on achieving challenging recruiting targets and recruits successfully completing the lengthy training process.

CASE STUDY NINE
Royal Air Force General Technician Electrical

1 Electrical specialists in the General Technician trade service and repair all types of electrically operated equipment used to support aircraft and ground operations. This can include ground power units for starting aircraft, portable generators, temporary electrical installations and vehicle electrical systems.

2 All new entrants into the General Technician Electrical trade are enrolled on an Advanced Apprenticeship.

- Phase 1 training – nine weeks. Common to all Royal Air Force recruits.

- Phase 2 training – 16 months, to gain key skills in basic trade training and complete a technical certificate, following which the recruit will be classified as 'Into Productive Service'. The Royal Air Force do not routinely collect information on the cost of recruiting and training individual trades. However the overall cost of recruiting and training a ground trade Airman to the point of 'Into Productive Service' is £98,000 (2004-05 figures).

- NVQ3 portfolio to be completed and assessed by the training school.

- 'Q-Ops' qualification is awarded once an individual has achieved both the level and range of competencies required, and completed a minimum of three years service.

- A recruit can be deployed once they have achieved the 'Q-Ops' qualification.

- The NVQ 3 along with the technical certificate and key skills achieved in basic training completes the criteria for the award of the Advanced Apprenticeship.

General Technician Electrical manning

3 The requirement for General Technician Electrical has reduced steadily over the last five years, and with increased efforts focussed on recruitment, the trade as at April 2006 was almost fully manned at an overall level – 605 personnel against a requirement of 615 personnel (1.6 per cent shortfall). However there were still shortages within the trade at Junior Technician, Senior Aircraftsman, and Leading Aircraftsman ranks, which together had only 91 per cent of the personnel required (as at November 2005). At the lower ranks there are a number of personnel who have not obtained the 'Q-Ops' qualification and are therefore technically unable to be deployed. As at September 2006, 61 out of 292 (21 per cent) General Technician Electrical Senior Aircraftsmen and Junior Technicians had not achieved 'Q-Ops'. A further 33 (11 per cent) were in training but not yet qualified.

Why is this trade an operational pinch point?

4 The General Technician Electrical trade is an operational pinch point due to increased commitments. The Royal Air Force has successfully recruited over 88 per cent of their target in the last five years, with the exception of 2003-04 where recruiting performance fell to 67 per cent of the target. Retention in the trade is also fairly healthy, and in the past few years the percentage of personnel choosing to leave early has been lower than the Airmen target exit rate of four per cent.

Operational commitments

5 Despite manning shortfalls at the lower ranks, operational commitments are met but this is largely due to the fact that General Technician Electrical personnel are sent on operations with greater frequency. The percentage of individuals exceeding 140 days separated service in a year has exceeded the target of 2.5 per cent of personnel since 1997-98. The percentage of individuals being sent on operations more frequently than the target tour interval of 16 months has increased in the last three years and was at 17 per cent as at March 2005 (**Figure 10**).

6 Posts in theatre are not allowed to be gapped and furthermore must be filled by an individual with the relevant skills. As such there is a heavier burden amongst deployable 'Q-Ops' personnel. There is a risk that with supervisors being deployed more frequently there is less supervisor training time and it may take trainees longer to gain their 'Q-Ops' status.

Initiatives in place

7 Given the problems within the trade group in terms of frequency of operational deployments and a shortage of fully deployable personnel, a waiver was approved to enable individuals nearing completion of the 'Q-Ops' qualification to deploy. This was introduced as a short term measure in August 2005 to ease pressure on those individuals having to deploy most frequently (Junior Technicians and Senior Aircraftsmen). The waiver has made a significant difference on the turn round time between operations. Junior Technicians and Senior Aircraftsmen have gone from being deployed every 12-16 months (in the period April 2004 to June 2005) to 30-36 months from October 2005 onwards. There may be risks allowing personnel to deploy before completing the necessary qualification.

8 A level of self-authorisation has also been introduced at the Junior Technician rank who are now able to self-check certain aspects of their work. This measure was introduced to reduce the burden on the more senior ranks.

9 Early work is underway looking at the optimum length of training and the possibility of aligning the trade name with civilian titles to make the trade more appealing to potential recruits.

Removal from the operational pinch point register

10 General Technician Electrical trade was removed from the operational pinch point register in 2006, as manning reached 99.2 per cent. Maintaining this manning level is of course dependent on voluntary outflow remaining low, achieving recruiting targets, and the requirement and demand for General Technician Electrical posts not being further increased.

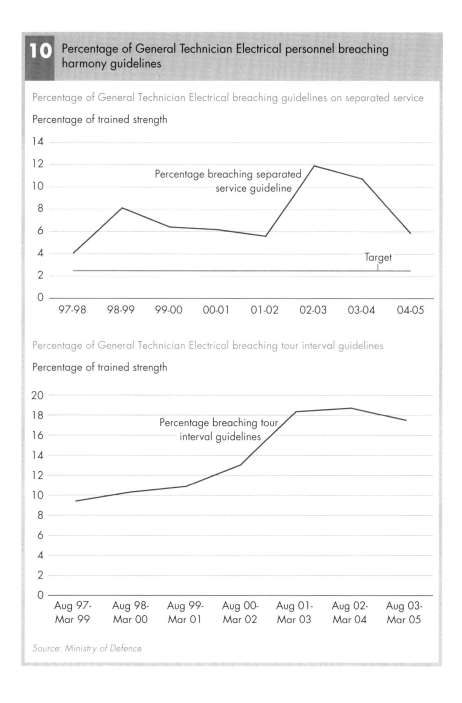

10 Percentage of General Technician Electrical personnel breaching harmony guidelines

Percentage of General Technician Electrical breaching guidelines on separated service

Percentage of trained strength

Percentage breaching separated service guideline

Target

97-98   98-99   99-00   00-01   01-02   02-03   03-04   04-05

Percentage of General Technician Electrical breaching tour interval guidelines

Percentage of trained strength

Percentage breaching tour interval guidelines

Aug 97-   Aug 98-   Aug 99-   Aug 00-   Aug 01-   Aug 02-   Aug 03-
Mar 99   Mar 00   Mar 01   Mar 02   Mar 03   Mar 04   Mar 05

Source: Ministry of Defence

CASE STUDY TEN
General Practitioners (Tri-Service)

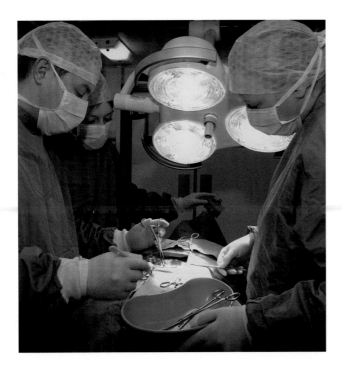

1 Medics[3] in all three Services provide crucial support for military personnel on operations abroad and contribute to the delivery of health care for both military and civilian personnel in the United Kingdom. Medical roles mirror in broad terms their civilian health care equivalents, with additional Service specific competencies required for some roles[4]. General Practitioners are Medical Officers,

caring for the personnel and families of his or her regiment or other Unit in the United Kingdom, as well as serving abroad and in Field Hospitals.

2 There are two main ways in which General Practitioners are recruited to the Services. The majority of General Practitioners come through the undergraduate route **(Figure 11)**.

11 General Practitioner entry routes	
Undergraduates	**Direct entry**
Recruited as undergraduate cadets	Already qualified as a General Practitioner, recruited either from the National Health Service, or private practice
Qualify from medical school	
Formally join the Armed Forces	
Entry Officer Course (4½ months) to learn military skills, Officer's duties and Service specific skills	Undergo military training and complete Entry Officer Course (4½ months)
Two to three years as 'general duties' Medical Officer (deployable during this time)	Deployable on operations
Several years postgraduate training towards becoming a fully qualified General Practitioner (time spent as 'general duties' doctor may count towards General Practitioner training)	

Source: National Audit Office

---

3   The term 'medic' is here used as a collective term for medical (doctors), clinical (nurses, Allied Health Professionals), and medical support (non-clinical roles) such as the Combat Medical Technician.

4   This includes expertise in underwater medicine, delivery of care onboard ship, radiation safety and atmosphere control for the Royal Navy, capability in aviation medicine and aeromedical evacuation for the Royal Air Force, and medical capability including paramedical skills and battlefield advanced trauma life support techniques for the Army.

General Practitioner manning

3   **Figure 12** shows the total trained strength against the Requirement. The numbers who are actually deployable will be different to the trained strength - some may not be deployable for medical reasons, or because they do not have up to date clinical skills.

4   As at June 2006, the Department were reporting a shortfall of 17 per cent against the requirement for accredited General Practitioners. The shortfalls vary in each Service. General Practitioner manning has been below requirement for the last five years, however manning has remained relatively stable, with a slight improvement over the last two years in all three Services.

5   Data on voluntary outflow is not available at the trade level for General Practitioners in all three Services.

Why is this trade an operational pinch point?

6   Up until the late 1990s Armed Forces medics worked in a more isolated environment in the former military hospitals. The 1994 'Defence Costs Study 15' instituted a substantial reduction in the manning requirement of the regular Defence Medical Services, and the closure of all but one of the former military hospitals, with an subsequent increase in reliance on Reserve medics.[5]

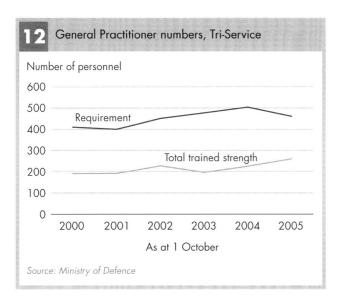

12   General Practitioner numbers, Tri-Service

Number of personnel

Requirement

Total trained strength

2000   2001   2002   2003   2004   2005

As at 1 October

Source: Ministry of Defence

7   The closure of the military hospitals means that medics in the Armed Forces now spend much of their time working in the United Kingdom alongside civilian colleagues in Ministry of Defence Hospital Units, attached to National Health Service Trusts. As a result, doctors and nurses are exposed to the competing terms and conditions of their colleagues in the National Health Service, and may find it easier to compare their situation unfavourably in certain circumstances. The recent drive to increase the capacity of the National Health Service has meant that Defence Medical Services are currently facing tough competition in the labour market for all types of health care personnel. General Practitioners are one of the trades which the Services have had difficulty both in attracting direct entry qualified recruits, and in keeping existing personnel.

8   General Practitioners and Medical Officers in the Armed Forces previously fared well in salary terms compared with their National Health Service counterparts, however recent changes to the General Practitioner contract now make it likely that a National Health Service General Practitioner will be at an advantage financially. The National Health Service system of remuneration means that General Practitioners in the Armed Forces will be paid on average £10,000 less than their National Health Service colleagues, according to estimates provided in the Armed Forces' Pay Review Body report.

9   The non-remunerative conditions under which General Practitioners work in the National Health Service may also be advantageous. The new National Health Service General Practitioner contract makes it possible for General Practitioners to choose not to provide out-of-hours care for their patients, an obligation which still exists for many General Practitioners in the Armed Forces. Some military General Practitioners may not see the families of service personnel, limiting the variety of medical casework in their practice.

10   There are some practical barriers to recruiting direct entry General Practitioners who are currently working in the National Health Service. Many General Practitioners are tied financially to their practices – they may have an equity stake in the practice, for example, which can make it inconvenient to leave. In addition, about 25 per cent work part-time and the numbers wishing to do this are increasing. A rising proportion of General Practitioners are women. General Practitioners may have family commitments which may make it impractical for them to work in a military context.

---

5   The precise manning requirements for future years have been reassessed as part of the Future Manpower Requirement of the Defence Medical Services study, completed during 2006. This review is likely to result in a reduction in the 'requirement' totals for the medical trades described in these appendices in the coming years, although details are not yet available.

11   Although in general recruiting direct entry qualified doctors and nurses has been challenging, recruitment of undergraduate cadets has been less problematic, with the Services generally being close to target for undergraduate doctors. However this will not necessarily help to tackle the General Practitioner pinch point, as there is no subsequent authority for the Services to direct medics to a particular specialism, and therefore limited ability to 'guide' these recruits to the pinch point trades where they are needed the most.

Operational commitments

12   Operational commitments are being met, however shortages of medical personnel mean that guidelines on separated service are being broken in some areas. Data on harmony guidelines is not available at trade level for General Practitioners in all three Services, however it is available for medical personnel as a whole. Around nine per cent of Royal Army Medical Corps personnel had breached the guidelines of 415 days separated service in 30 months (14.5 per cent of the Army on average) as at 31 December 2005, and between 0.5 and three per cent of Royal Air Force medical personnel had exceeded the Royal Air Force's guideline on individual separated service on average over the last five years. Medical personnel in the Royal Navy are not breaking harmony guidelines. This means that some posts may be gapped, however operational posts will be manned as a priority. As at 14 March 2006, 25.3 per cent of Royal Navy medical and nursing personnel (including dentists) were deployed.

13   Reserve Forces medics have increasingly being used in recent years in order to man deployments. For example, approximately 50 per cent of medics in Field Hospitals on Operation TELIC in Iraq have been provided by the Territorial Army. Medical and medical support personnel from coalition partners and from contractors have also been used to meet some commitments.

Initiatives in place

14   Financial incentives for medical personnel are being used to attract both direct entrant and undergraduate recruits.

15   Golden Hellos of £50,000 were offered for direct entry doctors in shortage specialisms, including for General Practitioners. The scheme ran from November 2002 to March 2006 and attracted a total of 36 General Practitioners from its inception compared to around four a year prior to the scheme being introduced. Army Medical Directorate expressed a concern that the pool of doctors likely to be attracted by such a scheme had now 'dried up'. £50,000 is not considered a large amount now in relation to typical General Practitioner salaries; furthermore, General Practitioners may be more satisfied with the current National Health Service contract than they were in 2002 when Golden Hellos were first introduced. However, the scheme is to continue in its present form and will be reviewed annually as part of the Armed Forces' Pay Review Body process.

16   For medical officers recruited as cadets, financial support is offered during the last three years of medical school up to an average of approximately £15,000 per annum for a return of service commitment of seven years following General Medical Council registration. Tuition fees are also paid for these three years at typically £1,200 per year (prior to the introduction of top-up fees). The Royal Air Force and Army also offer bursaries during the first two years at medical school of £4,000 and £1,000 per year respectively; in 2004-05 15 Royal Air Force bursaries and 10 Army bursaries were paid.

Retention initiatives

17   Pension arrangements in the Defence Medical
Services were changed in April 2005 to a system of
bonuses designed to reward medical and dental officers
to stay in the Services rather than take advantage of early
retirement (known as 'pay to stay'). Previously doctors who
were at least 38 years old and had completed 16 years of
service would have received an Immediate Pension if they
chose to leave the Services, comprising a lump sum and
annual payments depending on rank and length of service.
Since April 2005, new entrants (and from April 2006
existing medical and dental officers who choose to transfer
to the new system) will instead receive a series of taxable
bonus payments at critical career points, accompanied by
a five year return of service obligation. It is too early to say
whether this will prove retention positive.

18   The link between pay and rank, with medical and
nursing officers needing to obtain promotion through the
military ranks in order to obtain pay increases, has been a
problem. Many highly skilled practitioners may not have
the military or leadership skills composite with the rank
they would need to be in order to enjoy an equivalent
financial reward to their counterparts in the National
Health Service. In order to prevent medical officers
leaving the Defence Medical Services for this reason, two
pay spines were introduced in 2003 for the ranks from
Major to Colonel. These pay spines were disassociated
from rank, and were separately introduced for Consultants
and General Practitioners.

19   The Department is looking at the prospects for more
flexible working, including career breaks, home working,
sabbaticals, study leave and an ability to move easily from
the Regular to Reserve and vice versa. This work is still in
the developmental stage.

Removal from the operational pinch point register

20   It is likely that General Practitioners will remain on
the operational pinch point register until at least 2010,
although this could change once the results of the Future
Manpower Requirement study have been implemented.

CASE STUDY ELEVEN

Accident and Emergency and Intensive Therapy Unit Nurses (Tri-Service)

13 Specialist Nurse entry routes

Undergraduates

Join the Services as a Soldier/Rating

Complete 12 weeks basic military training

Complete three year University course leading to a nursing diploma or degree

Obtain registration with the Nursing and Midwifery council as a qualified nurse

Direct entry – two routes

Route 1

Nurses newly qualified with the Nursing and Midwifery council join as Soldiers/Ratings

Complete 12 week basic military training course, and are then deployable

Can apply for a commission to Officer after two years experience

Route 2

Nurses with two years post-qualification training can join as Nursing Officers.

Complete 12 weeks of Entry Officer training, and can then be deployed

■ Both Soldiers and Officers can take advantage of opportunities for further education and training after around two years of service post-qualification. Accident and Emergency and Intensive Therapy Unit nursing are two of the specialisms personnel can choose to train in, if they wish (specialist training can take a further two years).

Source: National Audit Office

1   Intensive Therapy Unit and Accident and Emergency Nurses are specialist registered nurses, who perform critical care nursing duties in the case of severe illness or injury.

2   There are two main ways in which nurses are recruited to the Services, with the majority coming through the undergraduate route **(Figure 13)**. For those who choose to train in Accident and Emergency and Intensive Therapy Unit nursing, the specialist nature of the roles means that it can take a long time to become fully trained and deployable.

Specialist Nurse manning

3 The graphs **(Figure 14)** show the total trained strength against the requirement. The numbers who are actually deployable will be different to the trained strength - some may not be deployable for medical reasons, or because they do not have up to date clinical skills.

4 At June 2006, the Department were reporting shortfalls of 68 per cent and 70 per cent for Accident and Emergency and Intensive Therapy Unit qualified nurses respectively. There are variations between the Services, but all have had shortages for the last few years. These are very specialist trades, whose small requirement means that large variations from year to year in percentage terms can result from small changes in absolute terms (only a few individuals joining or leaving), therefore caution needs to be exercised in trying to establish trends. Data on voluntary outflow is not available at the trade level for specialist nurses.

Why are these trades operational pinch points?

5 As noted with reference to General Practitioners, the manning requirement of the regular Defence Medical Services was sharply reduced during the late 1990s. The closure of the military hospitals during this period means that nurses in the Armed Forces now spend much of their time working in the United Kingdom alongside civilian colleagues in Ministry of Defence Hospital Units, attached to National Health Service Trusts. As a result, nurses are exposed to the competing terms and conditions of their colleagues in the National Health Service, and may find it easier to compare their situation unfavourably in certain circumstances. The recent drive to increase the capacity of the National Health Service has accentuated this, and Defence Medical Services are currently facing tough competition in the labour market for all types of health care personnel.

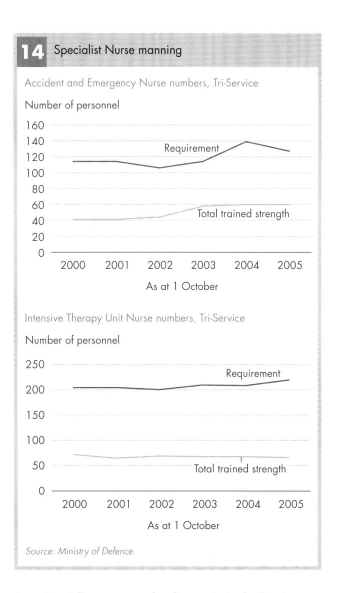

14 Specialist Nurse manning

Accident and Emergency Nurse numbers, Tri-Service

Source: Ministry of Defence

6 Specialist nurses are hard to retain in the Services. Their training and skills are highly marketable in the National Health Service, particularly given that it too has shortages of critical care nurses. The Services also find it difficult to recruit specialist nurses as direct entrants given the limited recruit pool, and are unable to offer some of the advantages of a National Health Service career, such as more flexible and family friendly working. Given the size of the overall trade group, the targets for direct entrants specialist nurses are very small, with only around one or two recruited in a typical year.

7   Basic pay for nurses in the Armed Forces has historically been higher than equivalent National Health Service remuneration. However opportunities to do paid overtime exist in the National Health Service and therefore few nurses will be on a basic rate. Furthermore, initial analyses by Defence Medical Services[6] of the effect of the new National Health Service payment system known as *Agenda for Change* on comparative pay indicates an increasing number of positions for which National Health Service pay is superior to the equivalent military rank, when proper account has been taken of allowances and benefits. The *Agenda for Change* reforms are still being rolled out and a final analysis of the effect of these changes is not yet possible.

8   Military nurses may have limited scope for promotion to a higher rank, and therefore higher pay, within their clinical area, as any such promotion must be based on a combination of merit and the availability of a post. Nurses may need to leave clinical work to gain the requisite military experience to progress up the ranks and advance their career, or they may choose to leave the Armed Forces altogether. This contrasts with opportunities in the National Health Service where, particularly under *Agenda for Change*, nurses who have acquired new skills may find it easier to achieve pay increases without facing the constraint of waiting for a particular post to become available.

9   Although in general recruiting direct entry qualified nurses has been challenging, recruitment of student nurses has been less problematic, with the Services generally hitting their targets for student nurses. However this will not necessarily help to tackle the main pinch points, as these recruits are not tied in to a particular specialism when they join. One of the main problems is persuading nurses to pursue a career in a particular under-manned specialism when they qualify. Recruits chosen specialisms may not be the ones which have the biggest under-manning problems, and the Services cannot compel medical personnel to train in these areas.

Operational commitments

10   Operational commitments are being met, however shortages of medical personnel mean that guidelines on separated service are being broken in some areas. Data on harmony guidelines is not available at trade level for specialist nurses in all three Services; however, it is available for medical personnel as a whole. Around eight per cent of Army Nursing Corps personnel had breached the guidelines of 415 days separated service in 30 months (14.5 per cent of the Army on average) as at 31 December 2005, and between 0.5 and three per cent of Royal Air Force medical personnel had exceeded the Royal Air Force's guideline on individual separated service on average over the last five years. Medical personnel in the Royal Navy are not breaking harmony guidelines. This means that some posts may be gapped, however operational posts will be manned as a priority. As at 14 March 2006, 25.3 per cent of Royal Navy medical and nursing personnel (including dentists) were deployed.

11   Reserve Forces medics have increasingly being used in recent years in order to man deployments. For example, approximately 50 per cent of medics in Field Hospitals on Operation TELIC in Iraq have been provided by the Territorial Army. Medical and medical support personnel from coalition partners and from contractors have also been used to meet some commitments.

Initiatives in place

12   Financial incentives for medical personnel are being used to attract both direct entrant and student/ undergraduate recruits.

13   Golden Hellos of £8,000 are offered for qualified Accident and Emergency and Intensive Therapy Unit Nurses. These have been less successful than the equivalent scheme for General Practitioners[7], with 11 awarded since the scheme began in January 2004. Defence Medical Services are reviewing the scheme and are considering whether the level of the Golden Hello should be significantly raised in order to increase the attractiveness of the scheme. Proposals will be made to the Armed Forces' Pay Review Body in 2007.

6   in their submission to the Armed Forces' Pay Review Body, 2006.
7   Armed Forces' Pay Review Body papers, October 2005.

14	Student nurses who have joined the Armed Forces are paid a wage of about £12-14,000 during their course in return for a three year return of service commitment on qualifying (in addition, bursaries are sometimes paid for those undertaking civilian courses).

15	Although bursaries and paid degree courses have proved successful at attracting students into military service, there is no subsequent authority for the Services to direct medics to a particular specialism, and therefore limited ability to 'guide' these recruits to the pinch point trades where they are needed the most, such as specialist nursing.

Retention initiatives

16	The link between pay and rank, with medical and nursing officers needing to obtain promotion through the military ranks in order to obtain pay increases, has been a problem and, as outlined in Case Study Ten, this link has been broken for some Consultants and General Practitioners. Nurses were, however, not subject to this change and senior nurses told us that similar provision would assist in retaining experienced nursing officers.

17	The Department is also considering targeted financial retention measures, involving a bonus system for nurses in pinch point specialisms (Intensive Therapy Unit, Emergency nursing and Operating Theatres), and those willing to commit to training in these pinch point areas. This would attract a return of service commitment within that specialism. The Department is also looking at the prospects for more flexible working, including career breaks, home working, sabbaticals, study leave and an ability to move easily from the Regular to Reserve and vice versa. This work is still in the developmental stage.

Removal from the operational pinch point register

18	It is likely that specialist nurses will remain on the operational pinch point register until at least 2010, although this could change once the results of the Future Manpower Requirement study have been implemented.

Printed in the UK for the Stationery Office Limited
on behalf of the Controller of Her Majesty's Stationery Office
5439850   11/06   77240